Broadcast Newswriting A WORKBOOK

Broadcast
Newswriting A WORKBOOK

K. TIM WULFEMEYER

Iowa State University Press / AMES

© 1983 Iowa State University Press, Ames, Iowa 50010

Manufactured in the United States of America

First edition, 1983
Second printing, 1989

International Standard Book Number: 0-8138-0226-1
Library of Congress Catalog Number: 82-883978

CONTENTS

INTRODUCTION

Writing news for broadcast is different from writing news for the print media. The audience doesn't have a written version of the broadcast news stories as they do with newspapers or magazines; therefore, broadcast newswriters must write in a way that ensures the audience will be able to understand complex issues and events on the first hearing and/or seeing.

Broadcast news must be written in a simple, direct manner. It must be written so a newscaster can read the copy easily and communicate effectively to people who often are not giving the newscaster their full attention.

The real key to effective broadcast newswriting is the ability to write the way people talk in their everyday conversations. Broadcast newswriters must strive to achieve an informal, conversational, flowing writing style. Ideally, newscasters should sound as if they're simply talking about issues and events with friends and not reading news copy to a faceless mass.

The information, examples, and exercises in this workbook are designed to help you begin to develop your skills in broadcast newswriting. At first you might find that trying to write the way people talk is rather difficult, because most of the writing you've done prior to this probably has been done for various print media. Don't lose heart though. Just keep practicing. It may take some time to master the art of broadcast newswriting, but with enough practice you can do it.

Unless your instructor tells you differently, when you work any assignment in this workbook, you're a radio or television newswriter for stations KCTI-AM and KCTI-TV. The stations are located in Midcity. Midcity could be a major city in any state and some facts about it are:

Facts about Midcity

Population: Approximately 950,000

Top executive officer: Mayor

Legislative body: Nine-member Board of Supervisors

Court system: Municipal Courts: civil cases involving amounts of no more than $5,000 and all criminal cases where the possible term of incarceration is one year or less. These criminal cases are called misdemeanors, petty misdemeanors, and violations.
Superior Courts: civil cases involving amounts of more than $5,000 and all criminal cases where the possible term of incarceration is more than one year. These criminal cases are called felonies.

Schools (public): Midcity Unified School District, kindergarten-twelfth grade, enrollment: 78,000

Higher education: Midcity University: enrollment approximately 20,000
Midcity Community College (two-year, vocational): enrollment approximately 10,000

PART I

KCTI Writing and Reporting Guidelines

1 / NEWSROOM TERMINOLOGY

You will hear the following terms used around the newsroom:

ACTUALITY: Taped comments from a news source; used in radio.

AIR PEOPLE: Those who read copy over the air: news announcers, news-casters. See also ON-AIR PEOPLE.

ANCHOR: Same as AIR PEOPLE, PERSONALITY, TALENT.

ASSIGNMENT EDITOR: Person who decides which stories will be covered and which reporters will cover them.

AUDIO TAPE: Magnetic tape used to record sound.

BACKTIMING: Exact timing of final newscast segment (story or stories) to ensure it is aired. If the final segment is 1:00, a newscaster must begin the final segment with exactly 1:00 remaining in the newscast. Often a newscaster must either read pad copy or dump material in order to begin the final segment at the precise time.

BREAKER: Unexpected news event. Examples: fire, traffic accident, plane crash.

BRIDGE: Transition between story elements, stories, or newscast segments.

BRIEFS: Short news stories; usually about :10 to :20 long.

CHARACTER GENERATOR: Computerlike machine used to superimpose letters, numbers, and words on a television screen.

CHROMAKEY: Electronic process used to insert visual material behind a television newscaster.

CHYRON (CHIRON): Brand of character generator.

COPY: News story written to be aired.

3

DATELINE: Geographic location of a news story; usually found at the beginning of wire-service stories. See also WIRE COPY.

ENG: Electronic News Gathering. Refers to the use of portable videotape equipment.

FEATURE: "Soft" or "lighter" news story such as a personality profile, restaurant review, or movie review. Used also to describe special segments, such as "Keeping Fit" and "Consumer Help Line." See also SOFT NEWS.

FILL COPY: News stories not expected to be aired but which could be if needed to fill unused newscast time.

GRAPHIC(S): Visual material that appears on the television screen: pictures, slides, charts, or supers.

HARD NEWS: Reports of timely and significant events and issues.

INTRO: Introduction. Lead-in to film or videotape story or recorded comments from a news source.

KEY: Term for CHROMAKEY.

KICKER: Final story of a newscast; usually humorous.

LEAD-IN: Introduction to an actuality, voicer, sound bite, or reporter package.

LINEUP: List of news stories and other materials in the order they are to be used in a newscast.

MATTE: Letters, numbers, and words superimposed on a television screen. Commonly referred to as SUPERS.

NATURAL SOUND: Actual noises recorded at the scene of a news event.

NEWSCASTER(S): Same as AIR PEOPLE.

ON-AIR PEOPLE: Same as AIR PEOPLE. Also called ON-AIR PERSONALITIES.

OPEN: Beginning music and/or announcer section of a newscast.

PAD COPY: Same as FILL COPY.

PERSONALITY: Same as AIR PEOPLE, ANCHOR, TALENT.

PERSONALITY FEATURE: Story that focuses on the life and times of one person. Sometimes called a PERSONALITY PROFILE.

PRESS RELEASE: Information sheet from a business, institution, or agency. Usually has a public relations function.

PRODUCER: Person responsible for content and organization of newscasts.

PROMPTER COPY: Copy prepared for teleprompter.

READER: News story that newscaster reads without actualities, film, or videotape. May include use of chromakey graphics.

REPORTER PACKAGE: News story in which reporter narration is coupled with taped comments from news sources. Film and videotape are used in packages for television news.

RIP-AND-READ: Reading wire copy on air without rewriting.

RUNDOWN: Same as LINEUP.

SHOT LIST: Chronological order of scenes in the final edited version of a film or videotape story.

SILENT-SOUND: Television news story that uses voice over and a sound bite or full-volume natural sound.

SOF: Sound On Film. Audio tape is bonded to film so audio and video are synchronized (in sync).

SOFT NEWS: Feature stories that usually are timeless.

SOT: Sound On Tape. Sound recorded in sync with picture on videotape.

SOUND BITE: Filmed or videotaped comments from a news source. Usually only the news source is seen in the film or videotape.

SOUND POP: Same as SOUND BITE.

SOURCE COPY: Material used as a basis for writing or rewriting a story for air. Includes wire copy, newspapers, and press releases.

SUPER: Same as MATTE.

TAG: Ending sentence or two, which an anchor reads following a voicer, reporter package, actuality, or sound bite.

TAG LINE: Final sentence or two spoken by a reporter in a package or voicer. Usually includes the geographic location of the events, the reporter's name, and the name of the station.

TAIL: Same as TAG.

TALENT: Same as AIR PEOPLE, PERSONALITY, ANCHOR.

TALKING HEAD: Same as SOUND BITE. Usually only the head of the news source is seen.

TAPE: Audio tape or videotape.

TEASE: Copy that precedes a commercial. Normally used to entice audience to stay tuned.

TELEPROMPTER: Device that allows television newscasters to read copy without having to look away from camera lens.

TOSS: Same as TEASE. Also used to refer to transitions between the comments of on-air personalities.

TRT: Total Running Time. Refers to length of story (first word to last word, including all actualities, voicers, sound bites, or packages).

VIDIFONT: Brand of character generator.

VIDEOTAPE: Magnetic tape used to record sound and picture in sync.

VISUAL(S): Material used to enhance a story, such as pictures, slides, supers, film, or videotape.

VOICER: Radio news story introduced by a newscaster but narrated by a reporter live or on tape.

WIRE COPY: Printed news stories provided over teletype by the Associated Press (AP) and United Press International (UPI) among others.

WRAPAROUND: Voicer or package that includes an actuality or sound bite sandwiched between segments of reporter narration.

ZIPPER: Same as KICKER.

2 / WRITING STYLE

REWRITING

    All news stories on KCTI stations will be REWRITTEN and not simply RETYPED from source copy. This means you must write stories in your own words. You won't last long here if you merely retype someone else's copy on our script paper.

    Rewriting should help make the information easier to understand and listen to. It should also help ensure that KCTI will have its own sound. KCTI should not sound like any of its competitors. Remember, most of our competitors will get the same source copy we get. We never want to run the risk of having our audience feel as if they've heard any of our stories in exactly the same words on another station.

    You should be able to give the same basic facts in a better, or at least a different, way. At the very least you should be able to make the copy sound more conversational.

    Rewriting can and often should involve more than merely rearranging words and phrases or employing different expressions of the same facts and ideas. You can update information and freshen it. You can check the facts to be sure they're still accurate. Finally, you can obtain new and/or additional facts, figures, and statements.

    Whatever you do, REWRITE. At KCTI, we NEVER rip-and-read.

CONVERSATIONAL STYLE

    Write the way you talk. KCTI demands a natural, conversational writing style. We want our on-air people to be able to give the news to our audience as if they were talking about the news with their friends.

    Use everyday words--simple, easily understood words. Use simple, direct, declarative sentences (subject--verb--object).

    EXAMPLE: (This was taken from a recent KCTI-AM script.)

Having been identified as a suspect by police, Maxwell was arrested

early this morning.

People don't really talk this way, do they? We shouldn't write this way. We should write the way people talk.

EXAMPLE: (A rewrite of the above example.)

Police arrested Maxwell early this morning.

EXAMPLE: (This was taken from wire copy.)

Reported cheating by 15 of 30 Midcity Police Department sergeants on promotional examinations given last week has led to the invalidation of the results and a rescheduling of the examinations for tomorrow.

Again, do you talk this way with your friends? If you don't, don't write this way. Write the way you talk.

EXAMPLE: (A rewrite of the above example.)

Thirty Midcity Police sergeants will have to take their promotion tests over again tomorrow because some of the officers apparently cheated on the tests last week.

Avoid beginning sentences with phrases and clauses. We rarely do in our everyday conversations, so we shouldn't in our news copy.

EXAMPLE: (From a recent KCTI-AM script.)

Waiting until he was sure he had enough votes for passage, Governor Sorenson sent his proposed budget to the State Senate this morning.

Would you talk this way with your friends? "Hi, Ed! Did you hear the latest? Waiting until he was sure he had enough votes for passage, Governor Sorenson sent his proposed budget to the State Senate this morning." Don't write this way if you wouldn't talk this way. Remember, we want our anchors to be able to sound as if they're TALKING with their friends, not READING to strangers.

EXAMPLE: (A rewrite of the above example.)

Governor Sorenson has sent his proposed budget to the State Senate,
but he waited until he was sure he had enough votes to get it passed.

Take a look at the following examples of sentences that start with
phrases and clauses and the rewrites of the sentences. Which SOUND better to you? Those that do are examples of how you should write for KCTI.

EXAMPLE: Before a packed house at Midcity University's Little
Theater, Professor Janet Keller announced her retirement tonight.

EXAMPLE: Midcity University Professor Janet Keller told a packed
house at the school's Little Theater tonight that she's going to
retire.

EXAMPLE: Delayed by heavy traffic and tired after a full day of
campaigning, Mayor Moore managed to attend his daughter's graduation
tonight.

EXAMPLE: Mayor Moore made it to his daughter's graduation tonight,
even though he campaigned all day and had to fight a traffic jam to
get there.

EXAMPLE: Although he says he can't think of a place he would rather
be than where he is, Midcity University President Philip Longley
will leave tomorrow to be interviewed for the position as president
of the University of Hawaii.

EXAMPLE: Midcity University President Philip Longley leaves
tomorrow to be interviewed for the job as president of the
University of Hawaii. Longley is going even though he says he's
happy right here in Midcity.

Keep your sentences short and to the point. Take a critical look at any sentence that runs longer than 20 words (three full lines of KCTI-AM copy or four full lines of KCTI-TV copy). We don't want our newscasters gasping for breath halfway through a sentence.

Break a long sentence into two or even three shorter ones. Delete redundant words. Don't be afraid to start a sentence with "and" or "but." We do it all the time in our conversations, so we should write that way, too.

EXAMPLE: Midcity University still doesn't have a new football

coach. But Athletic Director Jack Buckman says he hopes to make an

announcement sometime next week. And it looks as if the top choice

...Eric Daniels of UCLA...just might be the man.

TALK TO YOUR TYPEWRITER

Sometimes a sentence or a whole story will LOOK fine on paper, but when you say it aloud, it just doesn't SOUND fine. To improve your writing for SOUND, before you put a sentence on paper, say it aloud or to yourself. If it SOUNDS good, then put it on paper. If the sentence is a little rough, work with it until you think the audience will be able to understand it easily.

After you've finished writing your story, read it aloud. Record it if you have the opportunity. Listen to how it SOUNDS. Be sure it says what you want it to say. Be sure it's clear.

BREVITY

Be concise in your writing. Get to the news, explain why it's news and give the important details. Most of the time you'll be writing 15-second to 30-second stories, so you probably won't be able to include all the information about every story. Learn to live with this. Give as many of the significant facts as you can in the allotted time.

Broadcast news simply cannot give the in-depth information that the print media can. We don't have the time. This doesn't mean we can't cover the important news of the day, though. It just means we must be briefer in our coverage.

REASONS AND IMPACT

In your efforts to be brief, don't eliminate two of the most important pieces of information in any story--the reasons behind the actions and the impact the actions will have on our audience.

Our audience wants to know WHY things happen and HOW things are going to affect their lives. It's our job to find out these things and share them.

EXAMPLE: The Public Utilities Commission has okayed that four-point-two-million-dollar rate increase for Midcity Telephone.

If we stop with just the above information, we fail to give our audience the reasons behind the actions and the impact. We fail to share with them how the increase will affect them and why it is necessary.

EXAMPLE: The Public Utilities Commission has okayed a four-point-two-million-dollar rate increase for Midcity Telephone. That will mean a hike of about three-dollars a month for each local customer. Midcity Telephone says it needs the money to cover increased labor costs.

NAMES

You've heard the saying, "Names make news." Well, about every story you'll write will have at least one or two names in it. It's important that you spell every name correctly and include a pronunciation guide if necessary. Mispronouncing a name hurts our credibility.

If you come across an unusual name and are not sure how it should be pronounced, check with other members of the news staff and look through our names advisory lists before checking with associates of the person named in the story or with the person directly.

Once you know how to pronounce the name correctly, place a syllabized version of it above the correctly spelled version.

            (MA-drihd)
EXAMPLE: Jim Madrid.

            (Keye-moo-KEE)
EXAMPLE: Alice Kaimuki.

Use upper-case letters for the emphasized syllable and place the hyphenated syllabized version in parentheses. Use the United Press International Pronunciation Guide. It is included on the next page for your convenience.

UNITED PRESS INTERNATIONAL PRONUNCIATION GUIDE

VOWELS

A AY for long A as in mate
    A   for short A as in cat
    AI for nasal A as in air
    AH for short A as in father
    AW for broad A as in talk

E EE for long E as in meet
    EH for short E as in get
    UH for hollow E as in the
    AY for French long E with
        accent as in Pathé
    IH for E as in pretty
    EW for EW as in few
    E   for middle E as in per

I EYE for long I as in time
    EE for French long I as in
        machine
    IH for short I as in pity

O OH for long O as in note, or
        though
    AH for short O as in hot
    AW for broad O as in fought
    OO for O as in fool, or through
    U   for O as in foot
    OW for O as in how, or plough

U EW for long U as in mule
    OO for long U as in rule
    U   for middle U as in put
    UH for short U as in shut

CONSONANTS

K   for hard C as in cat
S   for soft C as in cease
SH for soft CH as in machine
CH for hard CH or TCH as in catch
Z   for hard S as in disease
S   for soft S as in sun
G   for hard G as in gang
J   for soft G as in general

At KCTI, we use the full first and last name of a person on the first reference, but only the last name on each additional reference. THIS APPLIES TO BOTH MEN AND WOMEN.

We usually DO NOT use middle names or initials of people unless a middle name or initial has become associated with a person's identity or he/she requests that we use one or the other.

EXAMPLE: Edward R. Murrow.

EXAMPLE: T. S. Eliot.

EXAMPLE: John F. Kennedy.

UNUSUAL WORDS

Include a pronunciation guide for unusual words, too! If you think a newscaster might have trouble with any word, you're better off including a phoneticized, syllabized version above the correctly spelled version.

Include a pronunciation guide every time the word is used if it is extremely difficult; however, for most words, a pronunciation guide on the first reference is all that is necessary.

IDENTIFICATION

KCTI uses three basic ways to identify one "John Smith" from another. It's important that we make it clear which "John Smith" in our community is in the news, especially if why he's in the news is a result of some crime, accident, or award. We want to be sure there is no confusion over which "John Smith" we're reporting about.

Title

The preferred way to identify a person is to include some title or job description, or a description of what it is that has made the person newsworthy. This information is generally included before the person's name, unless the title is extremely long (longer than one full line of radio copy or two full lines of television copy).

EXAMPLE: The Director of the Midcity Help Center, Gloria Perkins,

says most people have some kind of emotional problem.

We NEVER place an ordinary title after a name as is often done in newspapers.

EXAMPLE: Gloria Perkins, director of the Midcity Help Center, says

most people have some kind of emotional problem.

We do allow a modified "title-after-the-name" construction.

EXAMPLE: Gloria Perkins, who is the director of the Midcity Help

Center, says most people have some kind of emotional problem.

Another way to handle titles and names is to use the title by itself in one sentence and the name in the next sentence.

EXAMPLE: The Director of the Midcity Help Center says most people
have some kind of emotional problem.   Gloria Perkins says it's just
a sign of the times.

When you have an extremely long title, break it up to make it more
manageable.

EXAMPLE: The Chairman of Midcity Citizens Against Unlawful and
Unnatural Uses of Public Open Space Land and Recreational Areas,
Leonard McFadden, told the Board of Supervisors it should get tough
with land developers.

Rewritten this becomes:

EXAMPLE: The chairman of a local pro-open-space group says the
Board of Supervisors should get tough with land developers.   Leonard
McFadden is the head of Midcity Citizens Against Unlawful and
Unnatural Uses of Public Open Space Land and Recreational Areas.

Address
    Another way to identify people is to include their address.   We re-
port addresses in one of two ways.

EXAMPLE: Susan Lynn, who lives at 4521 Mast Avenue, finished first.

EXAMPLE: Susan Lynn, of 4521 Mast Avenue, finished first.

Age
    The third form of identification we use is a person's age.   We re-
port ages in one of three ways.

EXAMPLE: The winner was 20-year-old Susan Lynn.

EXAMPLE: The winner was Susan Lynn, who is 20-years-old.

EXAMPLE: The winner was Susan Lynn.   She is 20-years-old.

We use a person's age only if it is pertinent to the story (if the person is unusually young or old to be involved in whatever he or she is involved in); or if we can't determine either the address or the title of the person.

We NEVER use age in place of a first name or by itself.

EXAMPLE: The 20-year-old Lynn.

Complete identification (title, address, age) is often used in crime, accident, award, or prize stories. Use your own judgment for other stories.

We use identification on the first reference only. After that, only the person's last name is used. Again, this rule applies to BOTH MEN AND WOMEN.

ATTRIBUTION

Attribution is the "who says so" in sentences. It is the source of your information. We ALWAYS report attribution at the beginning of a sentence, because that's the way we report it in our everyday conversations. It's also important to let the audience know from the outset that our newscasters are reporting the opinions of others and not giving personal opinions.

EXAMPLE: Mayor Ronald Moore says too many local businesses are not

paying their fair share of taxes.

We NEVER report attribution in the middle of a sentence or at the end as is often done in newspapers.

EXAMPLE: Too many local businesses, Mayor Ronald Moore says, are

not paying their fair share of taxes.

EXAMPLE: Too many local businesses are not paying their fair share

of taxes, Mayor Ronald Moore says.

Attribution is not necessary in every sentence, but it is MANDATORY when a statement is clearly opinion, especially if it implies blame, or when it could be questionable. Whenever a piece of information is a known and indisputable fact, you don't need attribution.

Attribution Needed:

    EXAMPLE: American cars are inferior to Japanese cars.

    EXAMPLE: Most college athletes are excellent students.

    EXAMPLE: The oil companies are ripping-off the public.

Attribution Not Needed:

    EXAMPLE: A fire destroyed the Desert Oasis Hotel in Las Vegas.

    EXAMPLE: A small plane has crashed at the Midcity Airport.

    EXAMPLE: Three men died in a traffic accident in downtown Midcity.

    Don't worry about coming up with a lot of synonyms for "says" or
"said." Most of them have a tinge of editorial comment.

    EXAMPLE: Claims, asserts, declares, vows, exclaims, points out,

    discloses, warns, promises.

    "Says" or "said" are the simplest, most direct, and most conversa-
tional of all the attribution words. You can use "reports" or "reported,"
if you feel the need to vary your words of attribution. They are nearly
as objective and neutral as "says" and "said."
    NEVER use "states" or "stated." They're too stiff and formal. How
many times do you use "states" or "stated" in your everyday conversations? For that matter, how often do you use any attribution words
besides "says" or "said"?

    EXAMPLE: Melissa states we should go to the football game.

    EXAMPLE: Melissa asserts we should go to the football game.

    EXAMPLE: Melissa claims we should go to the football game.

    EXAMPLE: Melissa declares we should go to the football game.

    EXAMPLE: Melissa says we should go to the football game.

    Which of the above examples sounds more conversational to you? The
one that does is the one we'd use at KCTI.

QUOTES

When you want to quote a source in copy (without the use of an actuality or sound bite), it's usually best to paraphrase a source's words.

EXAMPLE: "Midcity desperately needs an anti-litter campaign,"

Councilwoman Melissa Wulf said.

Paraphrased this becomes:

EXAMPLE: Councilwoman Melissa Wulf says Midcity needs an

anti-litter program.

Direct quotes are difficult and awkward to handle in copy, but if you must quote a source exactly, be sure to let our audience know you're doing just that.

EXAMPLE: Councilwoman Melissa Wulf said, and we're quoting her

exactly...

EXAMPLE: Councilwoman Melissa Wulf says, and we're quoting now...

EXAMPLE: Councilwoman Melissa Wulf says, and these are her exact

words...

EXAMPLE: Councilwoman Melissa Wulf said, and this is the way she

expressed it...

Remember, our audience can't see quotation marks and we can't expect our newscasters to indicate a direct quote by changing the inflection in their voices.

NEVER use the old, "quote, unquote" method. It's too awkward and formal.

EXAMPLE: Councilwoman Melissa Wulf said, quote, Midcity desperately

needs an anti-litter campaign, unquote.

Most of the time, paraphrasing is the best way to handle comments from sources, but you should quote exactly when a statement is extremely controversial, complex, or unusually well expressed. In most cases, paraphrasing allows us to condense a source's words and we can often make his or her points more understandable. Be careful not to change the meaning of what a source is saying when you paraphrase, though. Keep the meaning; just improve the words.

CONTRACTIONS

Use contractions! They're informal and conversational. Instead of "it is," use "it's." Instead of "cannot," use "can't." Instead of "does not," use "doesn't." Instead of "they are," use "they're."

EXAMPLE: It's going to be a long week for the City Council if it

can't work out that charter revision snag this afternoon.

ADJECTIVES AND ADVERBS

Be careful when you use adjectives and adverbs. In fact, avoid them as much as possible. Often they are opinion words or value judgment words that are best left for editorials. Let your verbs add color and action to your writing.

When you do wish to describe something, keep it simple and direct. If the mayor delivers a five-minute speech, then write he delivered a five-minute speech. Don't write that he flawlessly delivered a hard-hitting, cleverly worded speech. What's hard-hitting, flawless, and cleverly worded to you might be soft, flawed, and sarcastic to our audience. You report what the mayor said and let our audience decide what adjectives and adverbs to attach to the mayor's words.

VERBS

Use present tense verbs whenever possible. They make our newscasts sound current and add snap. Of course, if using a past tense verb makes more sense, then do it. You might try the present perfect tense of the verb, though. It makes a sentence sound more current than using the past tense.

EXAMPLE: District Attorney Edward Whittler resigned today.

Using the present perfect tense:

EXAMPLE: District Attorney Edward Whittler has resigned.

Use active voice verbs instead of passive voice verbs. The active voice improves the flow of a newscast and makes it sound more immediate. The passive voice slows the flow. (Passive voice includes a past participle and some form of the verb be.)

EXAMPLE: Midcity University was awarded a 500-thousand-dollar grant

by the Ford Foundation.

Using the active voice:

EXAMPLE: The Ford Foundation has awarded a 500-thousand-dollar

grant to Midcity University.

You can often identify the passive voice by looking for a past perfect tense verb followed by the preposition "by" and a noun, or by an implied prepositional phrase.

EXAMPLE: was awarded (past perfect tense verb).

by the Ford Foundation (prepositional phrase).

NUMBERS
We write numbers so our newscasters can read them easily.
The numbers one through nine are written as words: one, two, three, four, five, six, seven, eight, nine.
The numbers 10 through 999 are written as arabic numerals: 10, 11, 12, 13...101...476...849...999.
Numbers greater than 999 are written using a combination of our two basic rules. We ALWAYS write out the words "hundred" (for numbers greater than 999), "thousand," "million," "billion."

EXAMPLE: 16-hundred or one-thousand-600 (NOT 1,600).

EXAMPLE: 15-million-11-thousand-and-35 (NOT 15,011,035).

EXAMPLE: 487-thousand-332 (NOT 487,332).

EXAMPLE: 23-thousand-157 (NOT 23,157).

Approximations
　　Round off numbers whenever precise figures are not necessary.
ALWAYS include an "approximation" word before giving the number to let
our audience know we're rounding it off.

　　　　EXAMPLE: about 25-thousand.

　　　　EXAMPLE: nearly 25-thousand.

　　　　EXAMPLE: just under 25-thousand.

　　There are other approximation words, of course. The important thing
is to be sure to use one of them when you round off numbers.

Fractions and Decimals
　　Spell out all fractions and decimals. Spell out the "point," too.

　　　　EXAMPLE: About three-fourths of the people surveyed say they like

　　the program.

　　　　EXAMPLE: About 75 percent of the people surveyed say they like the

　　program.

　　　　EXAMPLE: The group collected nearly 12-point-two-million dollars.

Ordinals
　　Use "st," "nd," "rd," "th" after numbers used in dates, addresses,
or whenever you want an ordinal.

　　　　EXAMPLE: Hartson moved to 4578 70th Street on June 22nd.

　　　　EXAMPLE: The Tigers will try for their 23rd straight win on May 31st.

　　ALWAYS spell out "first" as in June First or first place.

Exceptions
　　We have a few exceptions to our rules on numbers. Time of day
(hours and minutes), addresses, and phone numbers should be written using
numerals even if they are less than nine.

EXAMPLE: The phone number is 2-9-2-2-8-7-1.

EXAMPLE: He lives at 1-0-8-4-7 Ramsgate Drive.

EXAMPLE: The tipoff is set for 5:15 tonight.

SYMBOLS

We NEVER use such symbols as "$, %, &, ¢." We ALWAYS spell out the word.

EXAMPLE: dollars, percent, and, cents.

We NEVER use any of the common measurement abbreviations such as "in., yds., ft., °, lbs., gals." We ALWAYS spell out the word.

EXAMPLE: inches, yards, feet, degrees, pounds, gallons, liters,

meters, miles, ounces.

ABBREVIATIONS

We use few abbreviations of any kind. Our newscasters could have trouble reading them and our audience might not recognize them. In most cases, simply spell out the names of organizations and other commonly abbreviated words.

NEVER abbreviate the names of states or countries, days of the week, months, titles, address designations, or junior or senior. EXCEPTIONS: Dr., Mr., Mrs. are allowed.

The names of most organizations should be spelled out completely the first time they are used in a story. Each additional reference can be made with an abbreviation.

EXAMPLE: The National Organization for Women, which is also known

as NOW, will be meeting here over the weekend. NOW chapters from

every state will be represented.

EXAMPLE: The National Collegiate Athletic Association has a new

president. William Richardson says he plans some major revisions

in the N-C-A-A.

Some organizations have become so well known by their abbreviated titles that if you used the full name, our audience might not recognize

it. Some of these include: NATO (North Atlantic Treaty Organization),
Y-M-C-A (Young Men's Christian Association), NASA (National Aeronautic
and Space Administration), C-I-A (Central Intelligence Agency) and F-B-I
(Federal Bureau of Investigation).

There are others, of course, but be sure you're not taking too much
for granted when you use an abbreviated version of an organization's
name. If you're in doubt, give the full name the first time you mention
the organization and then use the abbreviated version for later refer-
ences.

INDIVIDUALLY VOICED ELEMENTS

Everything in your copy should be written EXACTLY the way you want a
newscaster to read it. If you want a letter or a number individually
voiced, be sure to capitalize it and to separate it from related numbers,
letters, or words by using hyphens: U-N, U-S, F-B-I, G-O-P, N-double-A-
C-P, C-P-A, M-P, C-I-A, U-S-C.

EXAMPLE: The number to call is 3-9-5-8-1-3-2.

EXAMPLE: The number to call is 3-9-5-81-32.

EXAMPLE: He used to live at 1-0-3-2-6 Hill Street.

EXAMPLE: He used to live at 103-26 Hill Street.

PUNCTUATION AND GRAMMAR

We follow the general rules of English grammar, spelling, punctuation, and capitalization.

For assistance in the use of the English language, see E. L.
Callihan, Grammar for Journalists, 3rd ed.; R. Thomas Berner, Language
Skills for Journalists; or any standard English textbook.

We do allow the substitution of three periods (...) for commas.
Three periods are less likely to be overlooked when a newscaster reads
copy.

EXAMPLE: The reasons for the cancellation were lack of time...lack

of money...and lack of interest.

TIME

WHEN events occur is often very important.

Be specific in your use of time, though. Use "this morning," "this
evening," "minutes ago," "this afternoon."

"Today is too general and it becomes tedious if every story has a

"today" in it, since most of the events we report on happen "today."
     For clarity, ALWAYS spell out the numbers you use with the word
"o'clock."

     EXAMPLE: one o'clock...two o'clock...nine o'clock...ten o'clock...

     eleven o'clock...twelve o'clock.

     If you want to write 11:30, for example, you can do it just that
way--11:30--or you can write it 11-30. Either way is acceptable.

     EXAMPLE: 5:22 OR 5-22.

     EXAMPLE: 10:10 OR 10-10.

     NEVER use "A.M." or "P.M." when you report time. Most people don't
use them in everyday conversations. Most people say "this afternoon,"
"tonight," "tomorrow night," and so on, so we should, too.

     EXAMPLE: The curtain goes up at eight tomorrow night.

     EXAMPLE: The accident happened just after four this morning.

     EXAMPLE: The concert starts at 2:30 this afternoon.

     When you're dealing with hours, minutes, and seconds, be sure to
follow our style guidelines for numbers and remember to spell out the
words that go along with the numbers.

     EXAMPLE: Webster finished in two-hours-10-minutes-and-24-seconds.

     EXAMPLE: The winning couple danced for 49-hours-eight-minutes-and-

     17-seconds.

EDITING
     We allow only minor editing of copy. Remember, we're trying to help
our newscasters read the copy easily, so we can't use all of the standard
copyediting symbols. We can't permit messy, marked up copy, either.
     Strikeovers are NOT permitted (the).
     We DO NOT USE a letter or word transposition symbol (𝑁) (⌐⌐⌐).
     We DO NOT USE a letter elimination symbol (𝓘).
     We DO NOT INSERT a letter within a word (‿ᴧ‿).

EXAMPLE: (DO NOT USE any of the following.)

strikeover.....broadcast.....introduction.....guilty not.....
considion.

If you make a mistake, black out the mistake and type or print the
correct version above or next to the mistake.

EXAMPLE: The new ~~seohll~~ school will cost five-million-dollars.

EXAMPLE: The new ~~sophll~~ *school* will cost five-million-dollars.

The following are examples of the ONLY editing marks we allow:

L   Separate into two words.

⌢   Eliminate the blacked out words.

⊥   Insert a word or words.

EXAMPLE: Lori Lynn will be in charge of the new unit.

EXAMPLE: Lori Lynn will be in charge ~~but no~~ of the new unit.

EXAMPLE: Lori Lynn will be in charge of the *new* unit.

We allow no more than TWO editing marks or corrections per line of
copy and no more than SIX editing marks or corrections per story. If you
have more than that, retype the entire story.

COPY PREPARATION
1. Use standard sheets of paper (8½ by 11 inches).
2. Type on one side only.
3. Double-space the copy.
4. Use upper-case and lower-case letters for all copy to be read
on air.
5. At KCTI-AM, we use a 65-space line (16 full lines = one minute).
6. At KCTI-TV, we use a 50-space line (20 full lines = one minute).
7. Indent five spaces from left margin for separate paragraphs.
8. Use separate sheets of paper for each story.
9. NEVER divide words or numbers or hyphenated phrases at the end
of a line and continue them on the next line. End each line with a
complete word.
10. NEVER break a sentence at the end of a page and continue it on
the following page. Always end a page with a complete sentence.
11. Slug each story in the upper left corner with a one-word or
two-word summary of what the story is about. Under the slug, list the
name of the writer and the date:

Jones Murder
Wulfemeyer
4/26/81

3 / STORY STRUCTURE

LEADS

The lead in a broadcast news story is like the headline for a newspaper story. It should grab interest. It should give the audience an idea of what the story is going to be about. It should set the tone for the story.

Emphasis Lead

For most stories you will use an emphasis lead, which will consist of the most important piece of information. It should be whatever you would say to a friend of yours if you ran into him or her on the street.

EXAMPLE: Hi, Lisa! Guess what happened today. Mayor Moore

resigned.

Mayor Moore's resignation is the most important piece of information. Leading with it emphasizes its significance. Most of the time you'll want to get the "who, what, where, when, and how" of each story in the first couple of sentences. The "why" is usually saved for later, because more time is needed to explain it fully. Don't forget to include the "why" for each story, though. It's important.

EXAMPLE: Three Midcity women died in a plane crash this morning.

EXAMPLE: The prime interest rate has gone up again.

EXAMPLE: Midcity University has a new football coach.

EXAMPLE: The rain continues to fall in Southern California.

EXAMPLE: The jury in the Alfred King case is still deadlocked.

Blanket Lead

The blanket lead is general instead of specific. It covers a number of separate but related pieces of information or stories.

EXAMPLE: The State Supreme Court ruled on four major cases this afternoon.

After you've let the audience know you're going to be talking about four separate cases, you can begin giving the details of each one.

EXAMPLE: Governor Sorenson outlined his new five-point plan to pump some life into downtown Midcity this morning. (Note: After the lead, give the details of each point.)

EXAMPLE: Five people died in traffic accidents over the weekend on Midcity streets. (Note: After the lead, give the details of each accident.)

EXAMPLE: The Board of Supervisors passed three new money-saving measures this afternoon. (Note: After the lead, give the details of each of the measures.)

Narrative Lead

In the narrative lead you start with the first thing that happened and proceed through the story reporting the events in the order they occurred. It's like telling a story. The narrative lead usually is reserved for light feature stories rather than more serious news events.

EXAMPLE: A local construction worker was tearing up some floorboards in an old house on the east side of town this afternoon when he saw something shining out of a crack in the foundation. Mark Warren picked up the object, brushed it off, and saw that it was an 1890 50-dollar gold piece.

He called us and asked if we'd find out how much it was worth. Well, we checked and it's valued at 75-thousand dollars.

Warren plans to take the next couple of days off to celebrate his discovery.

Notice in the above example how the name of the worker is delayed until the second sentence. His title (or job description) is used in the first sentence. This is a common technique in broadcast newswriting.

Question Lead

Avoid the question lead. It sounds too much like a commercial. Besides, if you ask a question, you may not like the answer. You may be encouraging audience members to tune us out.

EXAMPLE: Have you ever thought about going back to college?

The above lead will interest those who may have thought about going back to college, but all those who haven't thought about it will probably tune us out. We don't want that, so AVOID question leads.

Another reason for avoiding the use of question leads and questions of any sort at any time in your copy is that questions are often difficult to read well. Besides, questions usually aren't that conversational.

EXAMPLE: A movie studio in Midcity?

Would you start a conversation with one of your friends like this? Don't start a broadcast news story like this either.

Often writers will insert a question in copy and then give the answer immediately. AVOID this construction, too. Again, do you talk this way? Don't write this way then.

EXAMPLE: Does Midcity Telephone really need the rate increase?

Councilman Roger Hedgeman doesn't think so.

Verbless Lead

Sometimes you can omit a verb in a lead. Instead of starting with "There was" or "There is," just tell what happened.

EXAMPLE: Another traffic-related death in Midcity last night.

EXAMPLE: Lots of excitement at the Board of Supervisors meeting

today.

EXAMPLE: Two more hats in the political ring for mayor this evening.

EXAMPLE: Another big drug bust in East Midcity overnight.

EXAMPLE: More rain in the forecast for tomorrow.

Vague Lead

A lead is supposed to grab interest, but don't try to grab interest by being vague. Many writers think they'll increase audience attention and interest by a vague reference to an event or issue. This technique can backfire, though, especially if the audience confuses the new vague lead with the preceding story.

EXAMPLE: It wasn't his idea, but he's going along with it.

What if the above lead follows a story about the governor's analysis of a new tax-cut measure? Might not the audience become confused? Will audience members know the sentence is the lead for a new story and not connected with the story about the governor? Maybe not.

Besides, would you start a conversation with a friend like this? "Hi, Karen! It wasn't his idea, but he's going along with it."

Poor Karen will be wondering whose idea you're talking about, what the idea is, and why in the world you'd start a conversation with such a statement.

DO NOT use vague leads! Be clear and direct in your writing.

EXAMPLE: Governor Sorenson didn't come up with the idea for a new

Sports Stadium in Midcity, but he's going along with it.

BODY

Once you've written the lead, the rest of the story usually flows in a natural and logical manner. One way to organize a story is to think of it as a series of main points and supporting evidence.

You identify the main points of each story and then list the support- ing evidence for each of the points. Supporting evidence would include such things as quotes, comparisons, and statistics.

After starting with an "emphasis" or other kind of lead, list the appropriate supporting evidence for that point. Once you determine that you've covered the most significant point adequately, move on to the second most significant main point and the accompanying supporting evi- dence. Cover as many of the main points and appropriate supporting evi- dence as you can in the allotted time.

(Main Point)

EXAMPLE: Three Midcity Police officers pleaded innocent in Superior

Court this morning to charges of racketeering and assaulting a

federal agent.

(Evidence)

John Wood, Lester Fulton, and Marvin Katz are charged with

14 counts altogether. Most stem from an encounter two months ago

between the officers and a federal agent who was posing as a

pawnshop owner.

(Main point)

The officers were charged after a month-long investigation

turned up evidence of bribes and payments in connection with an

alleged protection scheme.

(Evidence)

The investigation involved F-B-I agents, Midcity Police,

and Midcity Sheriff's Deputies.

ENDINGS
     Ending a story can be almost as difficult as starting one. Most of
the time, though, you simply finish with the last bit of supporting evidence for your final main point.
     A great many stories can be ended by providing a piece of "back-
ground" information about the major person or persons or about the main
subject matter. Examples would include past accomplishments, related
actions or activities, and historical significance.
     You can end a story with information about what is going to happen
or what is likely to happen in the future. Finally, you can end a story
by telling the audience how to obtain more information about the major
issues, events, and people.

EXAMPLE: Kelly's first book came out in 1975.

EXAMPLE: Jones is also a member of the Society of Professional

Journalists.

EXAMPLE: Only five other tenured professors have ever been
dismissed in Midcity University's 50-year history.

EXAMPLE: Williamson will be arraigned tomorrow.

EXAMPLE: The bill now goes to the governor.

EXAMPLE: The Senate should vote on the measure sometime next week.

EXAMPLE: You can get more information by calling Midcity
University's College of Continuing Education.

4 / INTRODUCTIONS

ACTUALITY AND SOUND BITE

Introductions to radio actualities or filmed or videotaped sound bites serve two main purposes. The first, of course, is to grab the attention of the audience. The second is to prepare the audience for the information contained in the actuality or sound bite.

We use complete sentences for our introductions. By using complete sentences, we maintain a conversational flow in our newscasts. We also lessen the "egg on our face" if we have technical difficulties following an introduction.

EXAMPLE: Mayor Moore is against the program, because...

(TAPE)

IN: "We'd get cheated on..."

OUT: "...a lot cheaper elsewhere."
TIME: :20

If the actuality doesn't play, we can't recover as well as if we had used a complete sentence introduction.

EXAMPLE: Mayor Moore is against the program, because he thinks it

costs too much.

(TAPE)

IN: "We'd get cheated on..."

OUT: "...a lot cheaper elsewhere."
TIME: :20

The complete sentence introduction allows a newscaster to either ad-lib or simply continue with the rest of the scripted copy easier than the incomplete sentence introduction. A pause is natural after a sentence, so after realizing the tape will not play, our anchor can continue without necessarily having to explain why the actuality failed to materialize.

Avoid the "when asked if" method of introducing an actuality or sound bite. It has become a cliché in broadcast news.

EXAMPLE: When asked if he thought the program was worth the money,

Mayor Moore said . . .

(TAPE)

IN: "We'd cheated on..."
                                                              TIME: :20
OUT: "...a lot cheaper elsewhere."

Another thing to avoid is the "echo chamber." It occurs when the first words of the actuality or sound bite are exactly the same or very similar to the last words of the newscaster's introduction.

EXAMPLE: Governor Sorenson says it's time the state income tax was

reduced to a reasonable level.

(TAPE)

IN: "It's time the state income tax was reduced to a reasonable level."
                                                              TIME: :15
OUT: "...for all of us."

Instead of creating the "echo chamber," try to encourage the audi-ence to listen to the actuality or sound bite.

EXAMPLE: Governor Sorenson says taxpayers deserve a break.

(TAPE)

IN: "It's time the state..."
                                                              TIME: :15
OUT: "...for all of us."

REPORTER VOICER AND PACKAGE

Whenever possible, try to incorporate some aspect of the story in the introduction to a reporter voicer or package.

EXAMPLE: Lots of excitement at the Board of Education meeting this afternoon. And K-C-T-I reporter Jane Baxter was there for all of it.

EXAMPLE: More than five-thousand science fiction fanatics are in town for the National Convention of Science Fiction Anonymous.

K-C-T-I's Mark Zane sat in on the opening session.

Note: There's nothing wrong with the standard voicer/package introductions:

Jane Baxter reports.

Mark Zane has the details.

Jane Baxter has the story.

Mark Zane explains.

Do try to incorporate some aspect of the story in the introduction whenever you can logically do so, though.

5 / WRITING FOR FILM AND VIDEOTAPE

Writing for film and videotape requires much training and talent. Not only do you have to write in a conversational and interesting fashion, you also have to be sure that the words and pictures complement each other.

Two basic methods are used. In one the story is written to match scenes that are already edited; in the other the story is written first and the scenes are then edited to match the script.

Of course, whenever possible, it is best to coordinate the writing of the script and the editing of the film or videotape into one continuous process, but often we do not have time to do this. When you are asked to write a script for scenes that are already edited, first take a good look at the shot list so you will have an idea how to organize your script. You want to be sure your words will closely match what our audience will see.

Follow the "Writing Guidelines" below to help ensure audio and video matching. The effectiveness of our stories depends in part on how well the words and pictures go together.

WRITING GUIDELINES

1. Copy should flow in a natural, conversational, and interesting manner. Follow all our general rules and guidelines for effective broadcast newswriting.

2. Words and pictures should not conflict. What our audience sees is what it should hear about. Strive for a marriage of the visual and aural senses.

3. Avoid the "See Spot run. See Jane run. See Dick run." effect. You DON'T have to identify and describe EVERYTHING that appears or occurs in the film or tape. Film and tape will tell their own story in many cases. Instead of simply "describing" what the audience is seeing, "explain" the significance of what is being seen.

4. Be sure to identify each newsworthy person, place, or thing the first time they appear on the screen. We owe it to our audience to identify the major newsmakers, geographical locations, and objects.

5. If the film or tape has been previously edited, be sure to "underwrite" slightly. We want :03-:05 of film or tape after the

35

narration ends. If the tape runs :45, your copy should run between :40
and :42. We underwrite to be sure we avoid running out of film or tape
before we finish the narration.

EXAMPLES

    Flames (:03)   The fire caused about 185-thousand-dollars

                          damage.

    Smith (:06)   Fire Chief Jack Smith says the blaze started

                          when a smouldering cigarette ignited some old

    Trash can (:03)   newspapers in a trash can behind the store.

    Firemen (:03)   In all, 25 firemen battled the blaze.

    Cleanup (:06)   Cleanup operations lasted until five this evening.

    Valdez and project (:05)   The first prize went to Mark Valdez

                          of Santana High School. His project

    Chart (:04)   dealt with alternative energy sources

                          and their use in Midcity and surrounding

                          cities.

    McLissa and project (:04)   Jenelle McLissa of Woodrow Wilson

    Snail in enclosure (:09)   High School took second place. She

                          studied the reproductive cycle of the

                         common garden snail and how it compares

                         to that of freshwater snails.

                 ###

In the above examples, the scenes were included at the left of the
audio script to give you an idea of how the words and pictures should
complement each other.
    The KCTI script formats are included in Section 7 of this workbook
and specific methods for determining the length of the copy are discussed
in more detail then.

6 / NEWSCAST ORGANIZATION

Putting together a newscast is difficult. It takes imagination and creativity to pull together into a coherent newscast all the wire-service copy, actualities, press releases, rewrites, and reporter packages.

It also takes some organizational plan or model. If broadcast newscasts are thrown together haphazardly without any real order or plan, the result is a jumble of unrelated stories that usually has little meaning to an audience.

FORMATS

The continuity and flow of a newscast can be improved greatly by using a definite organizational model. You might use a number of traditional newscast formats, or you might want to incorporate elements of a number of the formats to develop your own. The important thing is to have a definite plan for organizing your newscast.

Four of the most commonly used formats are Chronological, Significance, Subject, and Geographical.

In the chronological format, stories are arranged in the order they occurred with the most recent coming first, followed by the second most recent, and so on.

In the significance format, stories are arranged in the order of their importance and impact for the audience. The story that affects the audience the most is aired first, followed by the second most important, and so on.

In the subject format, stories are grouped together according to topic. For example, all police action stories would be linked together, then all fire stories, all government stories, and so on.

In the geographical format, all local stories might run first, followed by state, regional, national, and international stories.

Of course, elements of the various formats can be blended and you can have much overlapping. For example, you might want to use the significance format, but might modify it slightly by giving the most important local news first followed by the most important state news and so on.

Do strive for SOME logical newscast organization, though. Our audience will appreciate it.

EXAMPLE: (If the following stories were available for a newscast,

you could put them together in different ways using the various

formats as models.)

1. Local traffic accident last night at 11 P.M. Two deaths.

2. Local house fire today at 2 P.M. Three deaths. $150,000 damage.

3. Los Angeles warehouse fire today at 9 A.M. Six deaths. $1.5
    million damage.

4. Local gasoline prices to go up 10% next week. Hike announced at
    3 P.M.

5. Midcity mayor appoints new member to Board of Supervisors at
    11 A.M. Appointment ends two-month search.

6. Strike at local defense plant. Started at 8 A.M. 2,500 workers
    affected.

7. President appoints new Secretary of State at 10 A.M. Appoint-
    ment is a surprise to most journalists and it ends a month-long
    search.

8. Strike by New York City garbage workers moves into second week.
    Story moves on wire at 7 A.M.

The stories might be aired using these various newscast organizational models:

CHRONOLOGICAL   SIGNIFICANCE

1. Gasoline prices   1. New Secretary of State

2. House fire   2. Gasoline prices

3. New supervisor   3. Local strike

4. New Secretary of State   4. New supervisor

5. Warehouse fire   5. Local fire

6. Local strike   6. Traffic accident

7. New York strike   7. New York strike

8. Traffic accident   8. Warehouse fire

SUBJECT	GEOGRAPHICAL
1. New Secretary of State	1. Gasoline prices
2. New supervisor	2. Local strike
3. Local strike	3. New supervisor
4. New York strike	4. House fire
5. House fire	5. Traffic accident
6. Warehouse fire	6. New Secretary of State
7. Traffic accident	7. New York strike
8. Gasoline prices	8. Warehouse fire

TRANSITIONS

Transitions between stories act as the strings that tie a newscast together. They should flow naturally. They should not be contrived. AVOID the "and speaking of" or "in other news" transitions. They are overused and provide no real link from one story to another.

Look for natural connections, natural links. If they're not present, then simply do without a transition. You don't have to have a transition between all stories. Just write them where they're appropriate.

EXAMPLE: (Transition between the appointment of the new Secretary

of State and the new supervisor.)

Back home...the search is over this evening for a new member for

Midcity's Board of Supervisors.

EXAMPLE: (Transition between the local strike and the New York

strike.)

Well, at least the strike at the defense plant isn't piling up

garbage like that strike in New York.

EXAMPLE: (Transition between the house fire and the warehouse fire.)

A warehouse fire in Los Angeles claimed twice as many lives and

caused 10 times as much damage as the one in Midcity.

7 / SCRIPT FORMATS

We've already gone over our general copy preparation guidelines, but it's important that you follow our various script formats. They are included on the next few pages. Follow the formats exactly.

RADIO

```
food stamps                                      TRT   :25
wulfemeyer
5/21/82
(reader)


     A new food stamp law takes effect next week.  It's

designed to stop some of the cheating, but local welfare

officials say it's so confusing they're not exactly sure how to

enforce it.

     The Director of the Midcity Welfare Department, Karen

Murphy, has sent a call to Washington for help.  She says it

will take an expert to decipher all the new regulations.

                            ###
```

Note: Remember, on KCTI-AM, we use a 65-space line. 16 full lines of 65 spaces each equals one minute of copy.

```
food stamps                                      TRT    :40
wulfemeyer
5/21/82
(actuality)


     A new food stamp law takes effect next week.  It's designed

to stop some of the cheating, but local welfare officials say

it's so confusing they're not exactly sure how to enforce it.

     The Director of the Midcity Welfare Department, Karen

Murphy, has sent a call to Washington for help.
```

```
                              (TAPE)

IN:   "We've asked the Department..."

                                                 TIME:    :26

OUT:  "...clear up the mess."
```

```
                               ###
```

Note: The "IN" consists of the first four words of the actuality and the
"OUT" consists of the last four words.
     Separate the "tape information" from the "anchor copy" by heavy
lines.

```
food stamps                                          TRT 1:00
wulfemeyer
5/21/82
(voicer)


    A new food stamp law takes effect next week.  It's designed

to stop some of the cheating, but local welfare officials say

it's so confusing they're not exactly sure how to enforce it.

    K-City's Lori McFadden reports on what's being done to

help work things out.
```

```
                            (TAPE)

IN:   "The Director of the..."

                                              TIME:    :45

OUT:  "...McFadden for K-City News."
```

```
                            ###
```

TELEVISION

```
food stamps                                      TRT  :25
mcfadden
5/21/82
(reader)


TALENT:                       A new food stamp law takes effect next week.

KEY:(FOOD STAMPS) It's designed to stop some of the cheating, but

                   local welfare officials say it's so confusing

                   they're not exactly sure how to enforce it.

                       The Director of the Midcity Welfare

                   Department, Karen Murphy, has sent a call to

                   Washington for help.  She says it will take an

                   expert to decipher all the new regulations.

                                   ###
```

Note: All video information and directions to the director should be
typed in all upper-case letters. All copy to be read on air should be
typed in upper- and lower-case letters.
    Copy to be read is ALWAYS on the right side of the script paper.
    Remember, we use a 50-space line for all copy to be read on KCTI-TV.
Each full line of 50 spaces equals three seconds.

```
food stamps                                    TRT   :35
mcfadden
5/21/82
(voice over)


TALENT:                    A new food stamp law takes effect next

                           week.  It's designed to stop some of the

                           cheating, but local welfare officials say it's

                           so confusing they're not exactly sure how to

                           enforce it.


TAKE SIL TAPE/VO           The Director of the Midcity Welfare

                           Department, Karen Murphy, has sent a call to

                           Washington for help.  She says it will take an

                           expert to decipher all the new regulations.

                               One thing is for certain, though.  Fewer

                           Midcity residents will be getting food stamps

                           under the new law.  In fact, Murphy predicts

                           about half the people who are eligible now,

                           won't be eligible under the new guidelines.


TALENT:                    The local welfare department hopes to have

                           the details of the new food stamp law available

                           for the public by the end of this week.

                                           ###
```

```
food stamps                                    TRT 1:15
mcfadden
5/21/82
(package)


TALENT:                    A new food stamp law takes effect next

KEY:(FOOD STAMPS)    week and K-City's Lori McFadden has found out

                     that the new law is causing some problems for

                     local welfare officials.


TAKE SOF              IN:  "The new law has..."

                                              TIME 1:05

                     OUT:  "...McFadden for K-City News."


                                ###
```

Note: Separate any change from the on-camera talent by heavy lines.

```
    food stamps                                        TRT  :28
    mcfadden
    5/21/82
    (slides/pictures)


    TALENT:                 A new food stamp law takes effect next

                            week, but local welfare officials aren't sure

                            they fully understand how to enforce it.
```

```
    TAKE SLIDE (MURPHY)     The Director of the Midcity Welfare

    FULL SCREEN             Department, Karen Murphy, says the new law is

                            so vague and complicated that she's asked the

                            U-S Department of Agriculture to send a

                            representative to Midcity to explain it.
```

```
    TALENT:                 The new food stamp law is supposed to

                            stop some of the cheating.

                                                        ###
```

Note: Use this format for any picture, slide, chart, or other visual that you want shown FULL SCREEN! Full screen refers to the visual filling the entire screen.

8/ REVIEW OF PART I

1. Rewrite all copy in your own words.

2. Write the way you talk. Use a conversational writing style.

3. Use simple, declarative sentences (subject--verb--object).

4. Keep your sentences short--about 20 words.

5. Write concisely.

6. Be sure to include the impact on the audience and the reasons behind the actions in all stories.

7. Include pronunciation guides for unusual names and words.

8. Place titles before names.

9. Place attribution at the beginning of sentences.

10. Use contractions.

11. Limit your use of adjectives and adverbs.

12. Verbs: use present tense and present perfect tense.

13. Use active voice verbs, whenever possible.

14. Spell out numbers one through nine. Use numerals for numbers 10-999. Write larger numbers by using a combination of the two rules. Spell out thousand, million, billion.

15. Spell out symbols.

16. Spell out abbreviations.

17. Use standard rules of punctuation and grammar.

18. Use the proper lead--emphasis, blanket, or narrative.

19. Structure your story as a series of main points and supporting evidence.

20. Use complete sentence introductions for actualities, voicers, sound bites, and reporter packages.

PART II

Writing Exercises

9 / STYLE TESTS

Use this example as a model for completing the style tests in this section.

(Original)

The new equipment will cost $59,872, Midcity Univ. Pres. Philip G.

Longley proclaimed.

(Rewrite)

Midcity University President Philip Longley says the new equipment

will cost about 60-thousand-dollars.

STYLE TEST #1

Rewrite these sentences in correct KCTI news style. Check your answers on pages 52 and 53.

1. Everyone knows 5% of two-hundred is ten.
2. The winner was Allan Jones, 56, 1254 E. 95 St.
3. Jane Peters, head of the judging committee, said the vote was sixteen-twelve.
4. The winning run was driven in by Howard P. Jackson.
5. Midcity University has been awarded a $1,009,500 grant from the Ford Foundation.
6. The new tax increase will be $5.8 million, Mayor Moore exclaimed.
7. Supervisor Maria Sanchez says it is possible we will not have the new buses by next year.
8. Sgt. April Stevens is the first female MP at Ft. Madison.
9. Atty. Terrance Shippen, 2324 Boston Ave., belongs to the NAACP.
10. The damage to the hotel was estimated at $200,000 by Fire Chief Jack Smith.

ANSWERS TO STYLE TEST #1

Look over the model answers and compare them to your rewrites. Be
sure to note the explanations for changes. The explanations are included
in parentheses following the rewrite.

1. Everyone knows 5% of two-hundred is ten.

1   Everyone knows five percent of 200 is 10.

        (Numbers one-nine are written as words; numbers 10-999 are
        written as arabic numerals; numbers larger than 999 are written
        using a combination of the two basic rules; spell out % and all
        other symbols.)

2. The winner was Allan Jones, 56, 1254 E. 95 St.

        The winner was 65-year-old Allan Jones of 12-54 East 95th
        Street.

        (Place ages before names; spell out "E." and most other abbre-
        viations; add "th" to 95 to make it an ordinal; spell out "St."
        and all other address designations.)

3. Jane Peters, head of the judging committee, said the vote was
    sixteen-twelve.

        The head of the judging committee, Jane Peters, says the vote
        was 16-to-12.

        (Place titles before names; use present tense of verbs whenever
        possible; use arabic numerals for numbers 10-999; place hyphens
        between individually voiced numbers and letters; write things
        EXACTLY the way you want them read on air.)

4. The winning run was driven in by Howard P. Jackson.

        Howard Jackson drove in the winning run.

        (Eliminate middle initials and middle names; use active voice
        verbs.)

5. Midcity University has been awarded a $1,009,500 grant from the
    Ford Foundation.

        The Ford Foundation has awarded a grant of just over
        one-million-dollars to Midcity University.

        (Use active voice verbs; spell out $ and all other symbols;
        spell out numbers one-nine; spell out "million"; round off
        numbers.)

6. The new tax increase will be $5.8 million, Mayor Moore ex-
claimed.

Mayor Moore says the new tax increase will be five-point-eight
million dollars.

(Place attribution first; spell out $; spell out "point.")

7. Supervisor Maria Sanchez says it is possible we will not have
the new buses by next year.

Supervisor Maria Sanchez says it's possible we won't have the
new buses by next year.

(Use contractions--"it's" for "it is" and "won't" for "will
not".)

8. Sgt. April Stevens is the first female MP at Ft. Madison.

Sergeant April Stevens is the first female M-P at Fort Madison.

(Spell out titles; place hyphens between individually voiced
letters and numbers.)

9. Atty. Terrance Shippen, 2324 Boston Ave., belongs to the NAACP.

Attorney Terrance Shippen of 23-24 Boston Avenue belongs to the
N-double-A-C-P.

(Spell out titles; spell out address designations; place
hyphens between individually voiced letters and numbers.)

10. The damage to the hotel was estimated at $200,000 by Fire Chief
Jack Smith.

Fire Chief Jack Smith estimated the damage to the hotel at
200-thousand-dollars.

(Use active voice verbs; spell out $ and all other symbols;
spell out "thousand, million, billion, trillion, etc.")

If you're not totally confident about your mastery of the KCTI style
guidelines, go back and reread the appropriate sections.

STYLE TEST #2

Rewrite these sentences in correct KCTI news style.

1. The new plant will employ 1,600 people, Mayor Moore promised.
2. The fire was caused by a short circuit, Capt. Robt. Tinker proclaimed.
3. Over thirty percent of all Americans fail to get enough exercise, according to a report by Harvard University.
4. The cost of the new museum was set at $14,980,900 by Gov. Sorenson.
5. The NCAA and the AAU are feuding again.
6. Jack Shelley, a professor of journalism at Midcity University, has been appointed to the FCC.
7. The two women got away with $151,230, Ellen Warner, president of American Savings and Loan, said.
8. Lt. Eric Overton will be the speaker at the ROTC luncheon.
9. Doris Willis, 70, 1898 Virginia Rd., was named "Grandma of the Year" today by the Associated Press.
10. Juan Lopez, president of Midcity Community College, announced his resignation effective June 21.

STYLE TEST #3

Rewrite these sentences in correct KCTI news style.

1. The cost of the new building will be $6,250,000, said Midcity Public Works Dir. Norman Tupperman.
2. Nancy Wolf, 29, 8753 N. Madison Ave., was arrested by Sgt. Sheila Yang.
3. The problem was caused by cheap gasoline, the mechanic reports.
4. A total of 7 people will share the $89,100 jackpot.
5. "Prof. Gilbert Wyatt is the worst instructor on campus," Prof. Ruth Tyler said.
6. Dr. Rachel Stein reports about 28% of all joggers suffer from the disease.
7. Wearing an attractive green dress, Sally Long, pres. of Midcity Furniture, Inc., opened the thirty-first annual convention of the National Freedom League.
8. Gov. Sorenson will not attend the "Candidates Forum" tonight at 8 P.M.
9. The Midcity Marathon will be run on Sept. 22, Mayor Moore stated.
10. The woman suffered multiple contusions and lacerations, Dep. Coroner Patricia Randolph exclaimed.

10 / COMPARATIVE LEADS AND BRIEFS

COMPARATIVE LEADS

COMPARATIVE LEADS #1

Indicate whether these leads are examples of emphasis (E), blanket (B), Narrative (N), or verbless (V) leads.

1. United Airlines is trying three new gimmicks to get   (E) (B) (N) (V)
   more people to fly the friendly skies.

2. A major new study has found that the so-called   (E) (B) (N) (V)
   "tracking" system used in many public schools
   hurts more students than it helps.

3. A local police officer probably wishes he'd stayed   (E) (B) (N) (V)
   in bed this morning instead of going to work.
   Officer Frank Woodward's problems started while he
   was getting dressed.

4. Midcity Vocational College President, Edward Prince,   (E) (B) (N) (V)
   has decided not to accept an offer to become the
   president of Fullerton Community College.

5. Another motorcycle-related death last night in   (E) (B) (N) (V)
   Midcity.

COMPARATIVE LEADS #2

Indicate whether these leads are examples of emphasis (E), blanket (B), narrative (N), or verbless (V) leads.

1. Another major brush fire in North Midcity this   (E) (B) (N) (V)

    morning.

2. The Board of Supervisors has approved four new city   (E) (B) (N) (V)

    charter amendments.

3. Governor Sorenson has proposed a five-point plan   (E) (B) (N) (V)

    to combat the state's rising crime rate.

4. Mayor Moore's day got off to an unusual start this   (E) (B) (N) (V)

    morning with a breakfast "roast" by the Midcity

    Kiwanis Club.

5. The price of ground beef should drop about   (E) (B) (N) (V)

    10-cents a pound next month.

COMPARATIVE BRIEFS

COMPARATIVE BRIEFS #1

Decide which example in the following pairs of briefs is written in broadcast news style.

1a.   William B. Bransford, 78, one of the world's longest surviving

heart transplant patients, died today in San Francisco. He received

a new heart on June 21, 1967.

1b.   One of the world's longest surviving heart transplant patients died

today in San Francisco. William Bransford was 78-years-old. He got

his new heart in June 1967.

(KEYE-roh)
2a.   Thousands of Egyptians rioted in Cairo and Alexandria last night.

Three people were killed and 38 were injured as the rioters stoned

buses, cars, and police. The rioters were upset over government-

ordered food price increases.

2b.   Three persons were killed and 38 injured as thousands of Egyptians,

angered by government-ordered food price increases, rioted last

night in Cairo and the port city of Alexandria, stoning buses,

cars, and police.

COMPARATIVE BRIEFS #2

Decide which example in the following pairs of briefs is written in broadcast news style.

1a.   A group of men armed with machine guns kidnapped a wealthy banana
                      (KEE-toh)   (Kas-TEE-oh)
      plantation owner in Quito, Ecuador, this afternoon. Jose Castillo

      is being held for 400-thousand-dollars.

1b.   Jose Lopez Castillo, a wealthy banana plantation owner in Quito,

      Ecuador, was kidnapped this afternoon by a group of men armed with

      machine guns. Castillo's ransom has been set at $400,000, police

      report.

2a.   The Midcity Liquor Commission is cracking down on topless bars in

      the downtown area. The commission has voted five-to-two to refuse

      to issue any more liquor licenses to bars that feature any form of

      nude entertainment.

2b.   The Midcity Liquor Commission set a moratorium on new liquor

      licenses for establishments in downtown Midcity which the commission

      identified as "nude bars." The commission voted 5-2 to deny liquor

      licenses to establishments that feature topless or bottomless danc-

      ing or any other form of nude entertainment.

COMPARATIVE BRIEFS #3

Decide which example in the following pairs of briefs is written in broadcast news style.

1a. About 50 nurses who are members of the Midcity Nurse's Association have threatened to go on strike at Midcity General Hospital next week unless their demands for an immediate wage increase of $100 per week are met. The nurses have been working without a contract for the past month.

1b. About 50 nurses at Midcity General plan to strike next week if they don't get an immediate 100-dollar a week raise. They've been working without a contract for a month.

2a. Trying to break up a student demonstration, riot police in Mexico City yesterday turned on bystanders, indiscriminately using tear gas against funeral marchers and schoolchildren. At least 25 persons were injured and 87 were arrested.

2b. A student demonstration in Mexico City got out of hand yesterday. Riot police who were trying to break up the demonstration started using tear gas on bystanders and schoolchildren. About 25 people were hurt and 87 were arrested.

11 / BRIEFS

Use this example as a model for the exercises in this section.

(Original)

Melissa Jenelle, 21, 10511 N. Pearl Ave., has been chosen "Home-coming Queen" at Midcity University. In addition to beauty, Miss Jenelle was chosen for her scholastic achievement and involvement in community and campus activities. Miss Jenelle is majoring in elementary education. She is a senior.

(Rewrite)

Midcity University has a new homecoming queen. She's 21-year-old
      (JEH-nehl)
Melissa Jenelle of 1-0-5-11 North Pearl Avenue. Jenelle is a senior

majoring in elementary education. She won the title for her beauty,

grades, and her involvement in community and campus activities.

BRIEFS #1

   Rewrite these newspaper-style briefs for broadcast.

(MIDCITY)--Scott F. Queen, 56, the personal photographer for former
President Richard M. Nixon, has been appointed to the State Board of
Industrial Review by Gov. John Sorenson. Queen will be in charge of
the photography section.

(MIDCITY)--A $3.25 million cancer research grant has been awarded to
the Midcity University School of Medicine, according to Dr. Theodore N.
Beetow, dean of the school. The money came from the Burton P. Maxwell
Foundation.

(MIDCITY)--Marshall James Marks, 6, died early today when he fell under
the rear wheels of a school bus, the county coroner's office reported.
Witnesses said the boy, son of Mr. and Mrs. James T. Marks, 1095 Mountain
Dr., started running along a curb as the bus approached and lost his
balance.

(MIDCITY)--Peter B. King, 44, Martin C. Krumm, 29, and Gregory L. Loo,
37, who, Midcity police believe, are suspects in 12 murders in various
Midwest states, were arrested this morning in an apartment at 2865 49th
St.

(MIDCITY)--A United Airlines jet with 109 persons aboard--including the
Midcity University varsity basketball team--made a safe landing at
Midcity Municipal Airport last night with one of its three engines shut
down, airport officials reported. An airline spokesman said the jet had
just taken off when a fire warning light came on. There was no fire,
however, just a malfunction in the light's electrical system.

BRIEFS #2

Rewrite these newspaper-style briefs for broadcast.

(NEW YORK)--After a prolonged illness, Adm. Walter N. Hyde, ret., 81,
former commander of the Atlantic Fleet Submarine Force, died here today
at Memorial General Hospital.
    Hyde was decorated several times during WWII.

(LOS ANGELES)--Dr. Doris E. Williams, 49, a professor of chemistry at
Midcity University, was injured in a two-car traffic accident here today.
She was taken to Harbor Medical Center suffering from multiple fractures
of her left leg.
    Doctors described her condition as good.

(AMES, IOWA)--Five persons were killed and 25 others injured here this
morning when a grain elevator exploded sending bits of metal flying as
far away as 2,600 feet.
    The cause of the explosion has not been determined.

(LAS VEGAS)--Fire destroyed part of the fashionable Desert Oasis Hotel
here this morning. No one was killed, but five firemen were injured
when a floor collapsed on them.
    Among the 500 persons who had to be evacuated was Ronald Moore,
mayor of Midcity. Moore was here attending the National Conference
of Mayors.
    The cause of the fire has not been determined.

(WASHINGTON, D.C.)--Susan L. Morton, chairwoman of the Midcity Board of
Supervisors, said today reorganization of the federal bureaucracy would
permit counties and cities to save time and money in applying for federal
grants.
    Morton expressed her views in meetings here before a Senate sub-
committee examining government red tape. There are too many unnecessary
forms and steps in the grant application process, according to Morton.

BRIEFS #3

Rewrite these newspaper-style briefs for broadcast.

(MIDCITY)--Harold L. Kettner, 47, was sworn in as the new police chief
of Midcity this morning. Kettner, a native of Midcity and a 25-year
veteran of the Midcity Police Department, replaces Bobby Joe Gray, 55,
who resigned last month after suffering a heart attack.

(HONOLULU)--Two persons died in a plane crash near here yesterday during
war games. A twin-engine Cessna 414 leased by the Pentagon crashed into
a hillside shortly after takeoff, according to a spokesman at Hickam Air
Force Base.
        The names of the dead were not released.

(MIDCITY)--An executive order declaring Midcity a disaster area in the
wake of last week's flooding was signed late last night by Gov. John
Sorenson. Homeowners who must rebuild damaged homes will now be eligible
for low-interest loans from the state.

(SANTA ANA, CAL.)--Leonard P. Dunn, 56, an unemployed disabled veteran,
who has now won three major consumer promotion games in the last 10
years, says he will use his latest windfall, a $25,000 prize, to buy a
new car and pay off some bills.
        Dunn bought a 45-cent soft drink at a McDonald's yesterday near his
home here, and correctly matched up four pictures on a game board.

(ST. LOUIS)--Using huge tank trucks and elaborate vacuumlike machines,
work crews labored all night last night to clean up crude oil that poured
into a southwest Missouri creek from a burst oil pipeline. Oil was
floating up to four inches deep on a three-mile stretch of Asher Creek
following the accident yesterday morning, authorities said.
        Officials expect cleanup operations to last at least three more
days.

12 / WRITING FOR RADIO

READER STORIES

Use this example as a model for the exercises in this section. The rewritten version of the original story is on the next page.

(Original)

Melissa Jenelle, 21, 10511 N. Pearl Ave., has been chosen "Homecoming Queen" at Midcity University. In addition to beauty, Miss Jenelle was chosen for her scholastic achievement and involvement in community and campus activities. Miss Jenelle is majoring in elementary education. She is a senior.

Miss Jenelle has a 3.4 GPA and serves as Vice-president of Kappa Alpha, a women's scholastic honorary society. With the selection, Miss Jenelle receives a $500 scholarship from the Associated Students of Midcity University, the student governmental organization

###

(Rewrite)

hc queen
jones
10/10/82

    Midcity University has a new homecoming queen. She's 21-year-old
    (JEH-nehl)
Melissa Jenelle, of 1-0-5-11 North Pearl Avenue. She won the title for

her beauty, grades, and her involvement in community and campus

activities.

    Jenelle is a senior majoring in elementary education. She has a

three-point-four grade point average and is the vice-president of a

women's scholastic society.

    Jenelle picks up a 500-dollar scholarship from the student

government for winning the title.

###

READER STORY #1

    Rewrite.   TRT   :20.

(MIDCITY)--Two men were killed early this morning when their car, a late model Pontiac, ran off Ruffin Ave. and flipped over, Midcity police reported.

    The names of the men have not been released pending notification of next of kin.

    Police said they suspect the driver of the car swerved to avoid something in the road, because there were 55 feet of skid marks leading to the spot where the car left the road.

    "The driver obviously just lost control of the car and couldn't keep it on the road," Sgt. Rhonda Sanders said.

    The fatalities were the 94th and 95th automobile-related deaths in the city this year.

READER STORY #2

    Rewrite.   TRT   :20.

(MIDCITY)--A 43-year-old resident of a downtown hotel was stabbed to death today after an argument with another resident, police reported.

    The victim, Lance M. Farley, of the Davenport Hotel, 206 Market St., was stabbed in the chest and back, Deputy Coroner Jack Larken said.

    A suspect, Franklin W. Smith, Jr., 46, also a resident of the Davenport Hotel, was booked into county jail on suspicion of murder.

    The two men argued about a debt Farley owed Smith, witnesses said.

READER STORY #3

    Rewrite.   TRT   :20.

(MIDCITY)--A fire believed to have been set caused $45,000 damage to a vacant house in Southeast Midcity last night. Investigators said a considerable amount of flammable fluid had been used to start the blaze.

    Two men were reported to have been in the structure shortly before the alarm was sounded at 10:20 P.M. The pair left the area by car, a witness said.

    Michael N. Francis, deputy fire chief, and firefighter James Rogers were treated at Midcity General Hospital for minor burns on their faces and necks.

READER STORY #4

Rewrite.   TRT :30.

(MIDCITY)--Police today are still seeking three young men who shot and
killed a Midcity woman late yesterday after spray-painting gang graffiti
on her home.

The victim, Mrs. Gloria Yates, 51, of 3620 Vista Ave., was struck in
the throat and upper chest by at least two bullets, Police Homicide Sgt.
Curtis Ring said.

Her husband, Frederick H. Yates, 53, declined to discuss the inci-
dent.

The couple was awakened about 11:42 P.M. by three men who were
spray-painting an exterior wall of the home.

While Yates was getting dressed, his wife went to a bathroom window
to watch the three.

The men sighted her and fired shots from a small-caliber weapon.

The phrase, "Outlaws Rule," was written on the wall.

Ring said there is such a gang in the Midcity area, but there is no
evidence that gang members were responsible for the shooting.

He also said there is no indication of why the home was singled out
for the spray-painting.

READER STORY #5

Write a radio news story from the following information (TRT :30):

Fire at "Tastee Donuts" store.
Address: 2358 Broadway (downtown).
Quote from Walter Anderson, Capt. Midcity Fire Dept.:
"I think it started when a pot of oil boiled over on the stove. It
was a hot one. The place was an inferno when we got here. We knew we
couldn't save the shop, so we concentrated on saving the businesses on
either side of it."

Shops next door--"April's Flowers" and "Maria's Earrings and Things"
--sustained only minor smoke damage.

Damage estimate to donut shop: $250,000 (building completely
destroyed).

Quote from Mildred E. Norton, 38, owner of "Tastee Donuts":
"It was my fault. All my fault. I forgot to turn off the stove
when I went out back for a cigarette."

No injuries reported.
Fire started about 4:00 A.M. (this morning).
Firemen left scene about 8:00 A.M.

READER STORY #6

    Rewrite.   TRT   :30.

(MIDCITY)--The third bank robbery in Midcity in three days occurred at
10:27 A.M. today when three men wearing motorcycle helmets and black
leather jackets robbed the Midcity Federal Savings and Loan branch at
1708 Garth Ave., according to a spokesman for the FBI here.

    An FBI official said one of the men was armed with a weapon de-
scribed by witnesses as a rifle or a shotgun. He said the trio fled in
a lime-green sports car.

    The amount taken was not disclosed.

    "The three of them swooped in here like the Daltons or somebody,"
Jason B. Beaton, bank vice-president, said. "It was like something right
out of one of those old-time westerns."

    A robber escaped on foot from the Bank of Midcity branch at 6542
Lakeland Blvd. yesterday and the Midcity Trust and Savings Bank at 2312
Merton St. was robbed by a man two days ago.

READER STORY #7

    Rewrite.   TRT   :45.

(LAS CRUCES, N.M.)--A funeral home here is suing Mountain Bell Telephone
Co. for listing the mortuary in the Yellow Pages under "Frozen Foods--
Wholesale."

    The $250,000 suit, by the Easy Rest Funeral Home, claims Bell did
not proofread the directory prior to publication and says it has been
"held up to public ridicule" since the misplaced listing appeared in this
year's directory.

    "We have received numerous crank calls over this," stated Jerry
Perez, director of the funeral home. "Some guy asked what our special of
the day was. Another asked if we sold only 'aged' meat. It's been
awful."

    Officials at Mountain Bell reported they cannot understand how the
mistake occurred.

    "We proofread our Yellow Pages at least nine times before distribu-
tion," claimed Mary K. Sparks, director of public relations for Mountain
Bell. "I just don't know how we missed it. It was an honest mistake,
though. We weren't trying to make fun of anyone."

    Mountain Bell plans to include an "Open Apology" letter to the Easy
Rest Funeral Home when telephone bills are sent out next month, according
to Sparks.

    The lawsuit is scheduled to be heard next month in a Las Cruces
Superior Court.

READER STORY #8

Write a radio news story from the following information (TRT :45):

Notes from a reporter:

Nurses at the city's five major hospitals could strike tomorrow.

Nurses, through their bargaining agent, the American Nurses Association, have submitted proposals calling for 20% annual pay hikes for the next two years, plus cost-of-living allowances of 10% per year.

Nurses presently make an average of $11.40 per hour at Midcity General, Midcity Memorial, Queen's, Kaiser, and Midcity Children's Hospitals.

About 1,100 nurses are involved.

Quote from Sandra Andrews, R.N., spokesperson for local ANA chapter:

"We're prepared to strike tomorrow if our proposals are not met in full by the negotiating team for the hospitals."

Hospitals' negotiating team is studying the proposals now. One member of the team (he asked not to be identified) said he thought the team would reject the proposals and come back with a counter offer at about 50% of the nurses' demands.

No official word expected from team for several hours.

The 5 hospitals have about 2,500 beds.

Average salary for nurses is $23,712 per year. If demands are met, salary would be $30,825 after one year and $40,072 at the end of the 2-year contract.

READER STORY #9

Rewrite.   TRT   1:00.

(MIDCITY)--School is out here for 78,110 students, but it is no vacation.
Midcity Unified School District teachers are on strike. There was picketing at all 65 city schools this morning.

At issue, as usual, is money. Midcity teachers claim they are the
poorest paid in the state. A check of salary schedules from the other
major school districts in the state confirms their allegation.

Arlene C. Simpson, president of the Midcity Teachers Association
(MTA), stated that her organization had asked for a 15% pay increase, but
had been offered only 8%.

"The administration's offer is a joke," Simpson said today in an
interview. "Even with a 15% increase we'll still only be able to keep up
with the cost of living. We'll still be the poorest paid teachers in the
state."

About 2,400 of the district's 2,559 teachers did not report for work
this morning.

Dist. Supt. Eric A. Otterman said he hopes to reopen the schools
tomorrow using administrators, teachers who refuse to strike, and whatever substitutes he can find. He also stated he will reduce the school
day from six hours to four hours.

"The district will not be embarrassed or pressured into paying more
than it can afford," Otterman said. "We are willing to discuss reasonable salary requests, but 15% is out of the question. Even the 8% increase will tax our budget."

Simpson added that the teachers are willing to continue picketing
schools and the district offices until their pay demands are met.

"We'll stay out as long as necessary to get what we rightfully
deserve," Simpson stated.

No negotiation sessions between the district and the teachers have
been scheduled.

READER STORY #10

Write a radio news story from the following information (TRT 1:00):
Traffic fatalities last night in Midcity (information obtained from Bill
Roberts, Midcity Police Public Information Officer):

(1) Local woman killed and husband injured in a collision involving
four vehicles on Interstate 15 about 12 miles north of downtown. Sharon
L. Richards, 21, was dead on arrival at Midcity General Hospital at
11:32 P.M. Her husband, Randolph J. Richards, 22, was hospitalized with
contusions and lacerations. He is in guarded condition. A police
spokesman said the Richards' 1980 Ford Mustang was hit by a southbound
motorhome after the Richards swerved out of the northbound lanes in an
effort to avoid two other cars that had collided. Nobody else was injured.

(2) George Norman Lafferty, 49, was pronounced dead at the scene of
a one-car accident in the 4700 block of Baily Ave. at 3 A.M. Lafferty
was driving west when the vehicle swerved right, climbed a steep embank-
ment, slipped back down, and rolled over. The driver was thrown from the
car.

(3) Donald Kiperts, 30, and Jane Kiperts, 27, his wife, were killed
when their pickup truck crashed into a telephone pole in a rural area
east of Midcity. Coroner reports they both died of multiple internal
injuries.

ADDRESSES: Richards, 9539 Ranger Rd.
Lafferty, 7761 Highdale Dr.
Kiperts, 10799 Jeremy Ave.
Deaths bring county total to 99 for the year.

ACTUALITY STORIES

Use this example as a model for the exercises in this section. The rewritten version is on the next page. Note that both an introduction and a tail are included.

(Original)

The Midcity Board of Supervisors has proposed a $150,000 cut in the budget for Midcity Childcare Centers. These centers serve 500 preschool children from low-income families. There are five centers in the city. The current budget is $450,000.

The supervisors think the $150,000 might be better used to help support a new after-school playground program.

Jane A. Reeger, director of Midcity Childcare Centers, is concerned about the proposed cuts. The cuts will mean 150 children will be forced out of the centers, she said.

REEGER actuality: Time :20

"The proposed cuts are ridiculous. We provide a valuable service. We help the kids to get ready for school and allow the parents to work or look for work. The proposed cuts will severely damage our program. The after-school program is fine, but I don't think it's as important as our program."

###

(Rewrite)

childcare cuts   TRT :45
gale
6/30/82

The director of the Midcity Childcare Centers is upset over

proposed cuts in her program. Jane Reeger doesn't think the Board of

Supervisors should cut 150-thousand-dollars from the centers and use

the money for that new after-school playground program.

(TAPE)

IN: "The proposed cuts are..."

                                                      TIME: :20

OUT: "...important as our program."

Right now, on a budget of 450-thousand-dollars, the centers serve

500 pre-school children from low-income families. But Reeger says if

her budget is cut, the centers will be able to handle just 350 children.

                                       ###

Note: Note how Reeger is identified before the actuality so the audience
will know who is speaking. Also note the complete sentence introduction
to the actuality. Remember, the actuality should flow easily from the
rest of your copy. It should be a logical continuation of your story.

ACTUALITY STORY #1

        Write a :15 introduction for the actuality from the
following information.   TRT :30

Information:

        Lt. Carl Mercer, spokesman for the Midcity Police Association (MPA),
warns that local officers will conduct a massive "sickout" next Monday to
protest the Midcity Board of Supervisors' refusal to grant officers a 15%
pay hike. Board has offered a 10% increase.
        Salary negotiations between the MPA and the board broke off last
night.
        Police have threatened to strike next month if their pay demands are
not met.

MERCER actuality: TIME :15

        "We have to do something to show we mean business. We just can't
accept the 10%. We need the full 15% just to keep up with inflation.
The average Midcity police officer makes only about $23,000 a year and
that just doesn't go too far these days."

ACTUALITY STORY #2

        Write a :20 introduction for the actuality and a :10 tail.
                                                               TRT :50

Information:

        Here's a switch! A doctor who is trying to keep patients away.
Dr. Donna Loren, one of Midcity's top plastic surgeons, says too many
people come to her asking for unnecessary or impossible surgery.
        In order to combat this problem, she has decided to offer weekend
seminars entitled, "What Plastic Surgery Can and Can't Do for You." The
seminars will be held from 9 A.M.-5 P.M. each Saturday for the next two
months at the Midcity Inn's Regal Room.
        Cost will be $10 per seminar; however, all of the seminars will be
the same, so a person needs only to attend one.
        More information can be obtained from Dr. Loren's office. Phone:
466-7788.

LOREN actuality: TIME :20

        "There's a lot of misinformation floating about concerning plastic
surgery. Some people actually think we can make them look just like
their favorite movie star. My seminars will be designed to give people
a realistic picture of what plastic surgery can and can't do. Plastic
surgery can help a lot of people, but it's definitely not for everybody."

VOICER INTRODUCTIONS

Use this example as a model for the exercises in this section. The rewritten version is on the next page. Note that both an introduction and a tail are included.

(Original)

Information:

About 125 postal workers picketed this morning outside the Post Office in downtown Midcity, 1284 Main Ave. Most carried signs. There was no confrontation, just a lot of shouting and name calling by both sides--workers and management--but police called by management officials. Police just watched from across the street. Negotiations to end 5-day strike are scheduled to resume next Monday. Management spokesperson reports mail will be delivered as usual by nonstriking workers and management personnel.

(Reporter Tim Daniels covered story and did a "voicer.")

VOICER IN: The picketers are upset about the overtime hours they're forced to work.

VOICER OUT: Tim Daniels for KCTI radio news.   TIME :45

#

(Rewrite)

postal strike   TRT 1:10
daniels
6/30/82

Postal workers were out in force this morning in downtown Midcity,

but they were picketing, not delivering the mail. K-C-T-I reporter

Tim Daniels went out to the picket line and found out what the commotion

was all about.

_____

(TAPE)

IN: "The picketers are upset..."
                                                                       TIME: :45
OUT: "...Daniels for KCTI radio news."

_____

Both sides have agreed to start negotiating again next Monday.

Meanwhile, we're still supposed to get our mail, because nonstriking

workers and management people are going to deliver it.

###

Note: Note how the introduction to the voicer incorporates an aspect of
reporter activity. It is not always appropriate to do this, but in this
case it works. Be sure to identify the reporter, though, before the
voicer. Audience members want to know who is doing the reporting.

VOICER #1

Write a :15 introduction for the reporter voicer included below. None of the information provided is included in the voicer. TRT 1:00

Information:

Midcity Board of Supervisors has approved the purchase of two parcels of land in the downtown area at a cost of $676,000 on which to build the Midcity Cultural Center (corner of Broadway and Main Streets).
    The purchase includes $327,000 for a 18,908 sq. ft. parcel owned by Shipstad Restaurants, Inc., and $249,000 for a 15,700 sq. ft. parcel owned by Midcity Federal Savings & Loan Association.
    Reporter Brenda Dunn worked on the story and did a voicer.

VOICER IN: The two pieces of land are all the city needed to complete the initial stages of the plan to build the cultural center.

VOICER OUT: Brenda Dunn for KCTI radio news.   TIME :45

VOICER #2

Write a :15 introduction for the reporter voicer below. Add a :15 tail after the voicer. None of the information provided is included in the voicer. TRT 1:30

Information:

Next semester Midcity University will be starting a new program to help students learn how to read better. It involves 5 classes, each with 15 students each semester for one year. Students will be enrolled in special classes if they score below 50% on the university's reading competency entrance test.
    Money for program will come from a $75,000 grant awarded to Dr. Robert Scott, professor of English at MU, by the National Humanities Institute. Program will run on an experimental basis for two semesters. If it is judged successful by the university, it will be made a permanent part of the MU curriculum, according to Scott.
    In the last freshman class, 25% of the students failed to reach the 50% level on the reading competency test, Scott said. He feels a score of 75% is really necessary for a person to be considered an average adult reader.
    Reporter Mike James did a voicer.

VOICER IN: MU officials hope the program will help get freshmen reading at a level where they will be able to understand college-level texts and novels.

VOICER OUT: Mike James for KCTI radio news.   TIME 1:00

NEWSCASTS

Rewrite the following nine stories to produce a four-minute radio newscast. Be sure to include appropriate transitions between stories.

Remember that 16 full lines of 65-spaces each equals approximately one minute of copy. For four minutes, you should have 64 full lines.

Each story should be typed on a separate sheet of paper. If you do this, you'll be able to rearrange your newscast easily. Be sure you slug each story and put your name on each sheet.

After you've rewritten enough copy to fill four minutes, arrange the stories in the order you'd want a newscaster on KCTI to read them. Number your pages in the lower left-hand corner, so that if someone drops the script or the pages get out of order, it will be easy to reassemble the script.

Be sure you submit the newscast to your instructor in the order you'd want the stories read on air.

Note: Include at least :30 (eight lines) of pad copy in your newscast. You should always prepare more copy and actualities than you think you will need. Your anchor might read faster than expected or there might be some technical difficulties with one or more of your tapes. It is always better to have too much copy than not enough. Play it safe. Include pad copy in every newscast. Normally, your pad copy will be a story of lesser significance than any other in your newscast. Label your pad copy clearly.

NEWSCAST #1

1A

(MIDCITY)--A Midcity-based consumer group, The Environmental Protection Organization, asked the federal government today to ban the sale of children's sleepwear containing the widely used fire retardant called "Tris," because it claims there is a "significant cancer hazard" connected with use of Tris.

"Nearly 100% of garments made of 100% polyester fabrics have been treated with Tris," William P. Bates, an EPO researcher, stated at a morning press conference.

"We have some data that suggest that Tris, which sometimes amounts to 10% of the weight of a treated garment, can be absorbed through the skin or if a child sucks or chews on the garment," Bates pronounced.

Apparently washing a garment five times significantly reduces the amount of the chemical, although some still remains, according to Bates.

1B

(DEMING, N.M.)--A motorist on Interstate 10 near here had an unusual explanation for two state troopers when he was stopped for weaving.

Glenn G. Broomler, Jr., told the troopers his pet boa constrictor
had gotten out of its cage and was slithering around in the car.

Trooper Marc Waxton and Trooper Supervisor Ronald Morren helped
Broomler recapture the snake, but apparently with varying degrees of
enthusiasm.

"Trooper Waxton says it (the snake) was six feet long, but he is
afraid of snakes," Morren said. "I say it was only four feet long, but
then I'm not afraid of snakes."

1C

(MIDCITY)--A Midcity man died last night when his motorcycle collided
with a pickup truck. Dead is Charles O. Sennett, 24, of 7621 Ramsgate
Blvd. Midcity Police say Sennett apparently lost control of his motorcycle and collided with a pickup truck on Magnolia Avenue about 11:50 P.M.

Sennett was pronounced dead on arrival at Midcity General Hospital.

Pamela T. Nater, 19, 4965 Haver St., the driver of the truck, was
not injured or cited.

1D

(DES MOINES)--Wives and husbands may enter voting booths together, a
State Administrative Law Judge ruled here today.

"The law is constitutional and must be followed," Judge John Edwards
said after reviewing the Iowa Conjugal Voting Bill, AB10985.

Edwards said the law did not violate the "secret ballot" concept,
which he called, "Sacred to all true Americans."

State Election Commission Chairperson, Karen L. Caster, said she
would instruct all Iowa counties to obey the law, but she asked, "What's
the difference between husband and wife voting together and brother and
sister, or boyfriend and girlfriend, or even employer and employee?"

The Iowa law also allows a voter to request assistance in voting
from a poll official.

1E

(MIDCITY)--Two men, one armed with a sawed-off shotgun, robbed a clothing
store here of approximately $2,517 in cash and two $250 suits last night,
police reported.

The robbery occurred shortly before 11 P.M. at Martin's Merchantile,
1722 Highland Ave., Lt. Gregory Craig said.

Teri Dantly, a saleswoman, said the men entered the store and
selected two suits from the racks. As she wrote up the bill, one of the
men pulled a shotgun and demanded the suits and the money.

Dantly said four customers and two other sales personnel were
ordered into dressing rooms as the robbers fled on foot.

Martin's was having an all night sale at the time of the robbery.

Police have no suspects in custody.

1F

M	U
S	D

NEWS RELEASE

Midcity Unified School District 4100 Normal Street, Midcity
                        Miles Milburn, Director of Public Information

TEST SCORES LEVEL OFF   For Immediate Release
   IN CITY SCHOOLS

    The annual decline in Midcity Unified School District comparative
test scores may have ebbed for the first time in over a decade, the Board
of Education was told today. The results of last year's testing of grade
6, 8, and 10 pupils show the scores held steady in comparison with national norms after over 10 years of decline, said Dr. Karl Ester, director of the district's evaluation services.
    "I'm not saying that we have solved our problems, but this is a most
encouraging sign," Ester said.
    The students took the Comprehensive Test of Basic Skills, which
Ester described as the most widely used test in the country. Each of the
three grades was tested in seven areas, giving 21 points of comparison
between the average student last year and the year before. Sixteen of
the comparison points showed exactly the same position relative to the
rest of the nation, three showed improved positions and two showed
declines.
    "It's really a super performance by our kids," Ester said.
    Taking the average student in the nation as the one who scores at
the 50th percentile rank, Midcity students scored above the national
average in 20 of the 21 comparison points. The only area below the
national average was 6th grade spelling, the report showed.

                                ###

MM:lw

1G

(MIDCITY)--Three Midcity supervisors maneuvered wheelchairs through an
obstacle course this afternoon in observance of the annual Midcity Handicapped Awareness Week.
    Jim Bates, Susan Morton, and Roger Hedgeman joined several other
city officials in efforts to dramatize the obstacles handicapped people
face each day such as: curbs, unevenly textured ground, and incorrectly
constructed ramps.
    The event took place at the Rehabilitation Institute of Midcity.

1H

(MIDCITY)--$.08. That's how much the price of milk (per half gallon) has
dropped in the Midcity area since the state decontrolled minimum retail
prices last Thursday.

MIDPIRG, a research group, yesterday reported 20 volunteer surveyors
checked prices at 27 major chain stores over the weekend. The report
showed Sav-Mor had cut prices the most.

Michael J. Jackson, co-director of MIDPIRG, said he does not expect
milk prices to drop much more, because state law prohibits retailers
from selling milk below cost.

Last year MIDPIRG (Midcity Public Interest Research Group) reported
a half gallon of whole milk was selling for $1.69. The $1.69 was the
minimum previously allowed by the state.

Over the weekend, MIDPIRG found the major chains had cut milk prices
$.08 to $1.61 per half gallon, except Sav-Mor where the price was $1.60
per half gallon.

MIDPIRG reported that smaller outlets were charging anywhere from
$1.63 to $1.75 per half gallon.

1I

(MIDCITY)--More than 38,000 students still have not been vaccinated for
rubeola measles, despite an intensive immunization program last week by
the Midcity Unified School District and the Midcity Health Department,
according to Donna Miller, director of MUSD nursing services.

Miller reports over 50% of district students were vaccinated last
week, 40,090, but 38,020 must still be immunized.

"From now on we will refer students to the health department or
their private physicians for their shots," Miller said.

According to Dr. Donald Shay, chief of acute communicable disease
control for the Midcity Health Department, there is plenty of vaccine.

"We need to get all students vaccinated, because we think we might
have an epidemic of 10-day rubeola measles this year if we don't,"
Shay said.

NEWSCAST #2

Create a five-minute radio newscast from the following 12 stories.
Be sure you REWRITE the copy. Don't just RETYPE it. Add some appropriate transitions, too. Include :45 (12 lines) of pad copy.

Slug each story and use separate sheets of paper for each story.
Number each page of your script after you've assembled it in the order
you want it read on air.

You should have a total of 80 full lines of 65 spaces each.

2A

(MIDCITY)--An early morning fire gutted the Midcity Boy's Club, 1797 Johnson Ave., causing damage estimated at up to $175,000, according to fire officials.

Officials said they suspect arson and are investigating the 2:10 A.M. blaze that also destroyed some new gymnastics equipment that had arrived just two days before.

Fire Captain Robt. Tinker reported the blaze appeared to have started in the upper office area.

"When we pulled up, flames were through the office roof and it was so hot you could hardly get inside," Nunn said. "Heavy roof tiles were falling in chunks. It was so hot it melted the Coke machine."

No injuries were reported.

Three engine companies and 17 firemen fought the fire for more than five hours.

"It's a total loss," Eugene Magee, club manager, said. "I don't know what our 257 members are going to do now that the building is destroyed. I guess we will just have to look for another building. I don't know where we're going to get the money, though."

2B

(MIDCITY)--A family argument involving several persons was blamed for the shooting death last night of Raymond Rayburn, 38, 2020 Norton Ave., shortly after 2 A.M.

Booked on suspicion of murder was William W. Taite, 62, 4581 Pixley Dr., the victim's father-in-law.

Witnesses said Taite, Taite's son, Timothy, and Rayburn began arguing over family financial matters. Rayburn reportedly pushed the elder Taite to the floor of the Ox Tail bar, 1675 Main St., after a brief scuffle. Taite left the bar, but returned a few minutes later waving a gun.

Witnesses said Taite walked over to Rayburn, who was sitting with his wife, Catherine, 35, uttered a number of obscenities, and fired two shots into Rayburn's chest.

Rayburn died on the operating table at Midcity General Hospital.

2C

(LOS ANGELES)--FedMart Corp., an ailing chain of discount food and general merchandise stores in the Southwest, said today that it will permanently close all its stores over the next several months, throwing more than 10,000 company employees out of work.

The announcement was made in a letter to workers at FedMart's 56 stores by Walter J. Heen, president of the Los Angeles-based company. "Under current economic and labor conditions, it was the only choice possible," Heen said in the letter.

A retailing industry analyst said the recession, rising unemployment, high interest rates and high unionized employee wages have been particularly hard on discount retailers, such as FedMart, which generally depend on less-affluent customers.

Most of FedMart's 56 stores are in Southern California. The company also has stores in Arizona, Nevada, and New Mexico.

2D

(WASHINGTON, D.C.)--The nation's largest steel producers, US Steel, Bethlehem Steel, Inland Steel, and Wheeling-Pittsburgh Steel, announced late last night that they have decided to delay a 5.5% price increase that was scheduled to take effect the first of next month.

Industry sources say some increases will surely come some time within the next year, but no specific date or new amount has been announced.

2E

(MIDCITY)--The vice-president of the Ohio College of Technology has been named the new president of Midcity Community College, filling the leadership position there which has been open for 18 months.

The appointment of H. H. "Buck" Wolff, who had served at OCT for 6 years, was announced yesterday at an open meeting of MCC faculty, staff, administrators and students, a college spokesman said.

Wolff, 45, will assume his new duties next month at the five-year-old private college. His appointment ended a search of more than one year for a president to succeed Dr. Willard Bleyer, 63, who resigned 18 months ago for health reasons.

Wolff earned his Ph.D. in economics at Purdue University in Indiana.

2F

(MIAMI, FLA.)--Daniel and Elena Zimmer have been married three times--to each other, that is--in four months, but the couple still isn't together. It seems government red tape is keeping the bride at her home in Lima, Peru, and forcing the bridegroom to resume the life of a bachelor here.

"Sure, I miss Elena," Zimmer said. "Hearing her voice on the phone is okay, but it's not like being married, if you know what I mean. We love each other and all we want is to be together."

Zimmer, a grocery clerk, and Elena were first married aboard the Blissful Voyage, a Miami-based oceanliner, but Zimmer said his parents wanted a church wedding, so the couple married again.

On the honeymoon, Elena decided she wanted to be married in Lima so her family could attend. Zimmer, 23, agreed, but after a large church wedding and reception, which was attended by several high-ranking Peruvian governmental officials, the former Elena Villa, 21, found that being the wife of an American citizen did not help solve a snafu in getting U.S. immigration officials to grant her a visa.

James O'Keefe, district director of the U.S. Immigration office here, said he did not know what was causing the delay, but he gave his sympathies to Zimmer.

2G

(MIDCITY)--Twenty-six persons, most of them students from a Midcity high school, were injured yesterday when a large truck driven by a Midcity man collided with the rear of a school bus en route to an outing at the Midcity Zoo, the Midcity Police reported.

Officers said the accident occurred at 7:55 A.M. on Interstate 5 about three miles north of the zoo when a semi-trailer truck struck the rear of the bus from Western High School.

The bus, driven by Alonzo J. Castro, 39, carried 56 students and 6 chaperones. The truck was driven by Stephen F. Nelson, 27, 8548 N. Mound St.

Both drivers were injured in the collision, but the injuries were not serious. The drivers and the other slightly injured students and chaperones were treated at Midcity Community Hospital and released.

Nelson was cited for following another vehicle at an unsafe distance.

2H

<u>NEWS RELEASE</u>

TO: Midcity Media

FROM: Midcity District Attorney's Office

                                        FOR IMMEDIATE RELEASE

    District Attorney Edward Whittler has proposed that a task force be
formed to review local election ordinances and to suggest amendments if
necessary.
    In a letter to the Board of Supervisors, Whittler said he thought an
investigation was necessary in light of last week's indictments of two
former officials of a local construction company for violating campaign
ordinances by allegedly making corporate contributions to the campaign
committee of Supervisor Linda Anderson.
    Whittler suggested the task force include representatives of the
Board of Supervisors, district attorney, registrar of voters, city clerk,
Common Cause, and the League of Women Voters.
    Among the areas Whittler suggested be reviewed are the effectiveness
and level of campaign contribution limitations, the effectiveness of pro-
hibitions against organization contributions, and the advisability of
imposing separate controls on officeholder's off-year political funds.
    "We've got to clean up some of the loose ends and loopholes or we're
in for some real problems," Whittler said. "I think now is a good time
to do it."

EW:ty

2I

<u>NEWS RELEASE</u>

TO: Midcity Media

FROM: Office of Public Affairs, Midcity

SUBJECT: Midcity Stadium Noise Control

FOR IMMEDIATE RELEASE

Paul M. Gade, Midcity Noise Abatement Officer, will recommend that the Midcity Board of Supervisors invest in a $19,875 device that would automatically govern the amplification of music played at Midcity Stadium so as to conform with the city's noise control law.

Gade calls the device a novel way to muffle the sound level of rock concerts at the stadium.

"It's not going to suddenly shut off the sound, though," Gade said.

Gade plans to recommend installation of the device when he appears before the board's Public Facilities and Recreation Committee next Tuesday night.

Rock groups would pay a small fee for the use of the gadget.

"We don't want to ruin rock concerts for the people who enjoy them," said Gade. "We just want to tone down the noise a bit and protect the rights of the nonrock lovers."

Gade said his office received more than 50 complaints from Midcity Stadium neighbors after the recent "Heavy Metal" concert. The group used 36 amplifiers and attained a decibel level well above that permitted in the city's noise regulations, stated Gade.

Gade believes monitoring the power supply of rock musicians to regulate the output of decibels is the only way to save the ears and windows of persons living near the stadium.

Several communities in other states use the device, known as the "Noise Capper," according to Gade.

HO:bb

2J

(MIDCITY)--A legal bid to have a Midcity chain store take down signs
labeling certain toys "boys toys" and others "girls toys" was argued this
morning before Superior Court Judge Milton R. Thompson, who took under
submission the class action suit against Buy-Rite Drug Stores, Inc.

"The issue is children's mental health," said Gloria Sakamoto, attorney for the plaintiffs: seven children and the Women's Equal Rights
Legal Defense and Education Fund.

She said that by putting dolls and cookware in an aisle labeled
"girls toys," and play money and tools in an aisle designated "boys
toys," Buy-Rite perpetuates sexual stereotyping, which is unfair.

Sakamoto said she was particularly angered by Buy-Rite's argument
that the designations were justified by the genetic differences between
boys and girls.

Buy-Rite Attorney, John J. Torgerson, said the practice of labeling
the toys was a "time-saving device" meant to assist customers.

The hearing on the suit continues tomorrow morning.

2K

(MIDCITY)--Sarah Jane Tippler, 18, 1745 Washington Ave., was pronounced
dead at the scene of a one-car crash at the corner of Mercer Street and
Oak Avenue last night at 11:50 P.M. that also critically injured her
passenger, Arnold C. Curran, 19, 3589 Oak Ave. Curran is undergoing
treatment at Midcity General Hospital.

Tippler was driving west in the 3300 block of Oak Avenue when she
apparently lost control of her car and rammed into a telephone pole,
according to Midcity police spokesperson, Marsha Whittmer.

2L

(LOS ANGELES)--A fire destroyed the famed Bonaventure Hotel here yesterday. Three elderly residents were killed and 42 persons were injured in
the three-alarm blaze.

Firemen battled the fire for nine hours before controlling it. No
other buildings were affected.

"We're not positive about the cause of the fire yet, but it looks as
if it probably was started by some faulty wiring in the kitchen area,"
said Los Angeles Fire Department Capt. Stephen P. Acker.

Damage estimates have been set at $12,000,000.

All the victims died from smoke inhalation. Many of the injured
suffered burns as they raced through flames which at times reached as
high as 10 feet. More than 350 persons had to be evacuated.

NEWSCAST #3

Use the following 12 stories to produce a five-minute radio newscast. Include :45 (12 lines) of pad copy. Be sure to include appropriate transitions between stories.

Two actuality stories and one voicer are included. Be sure you add the tape times and script times together to fill the five minutes.

Submit the newscast to your instructor in the order you'd want the stories read on air.

3A

(MIDCITY)--A local bar was robbed early today by four masked men armed with shotguns and pistols who shot open the safe after the bartender refused to give up the key, police said. The robbers escaped on foot with an undisclosed amount of cash.

The bartender, Stacy Gale, 23, 9841 Mercer Ave., was kicked in the stomach when she failed to provide the key to the safe in the back room, police said.

After taking wallets from Gale and the sole customer in the establishment, Sally's Saloon, 2959 Broadway, three of the men started to leave the bar, but the fourth returned to the back room.

"I'm going to shoot this sucker open, man. There's got to be a gold mine in here," the robber was quoted as saying.

Police said the robber fired three shots with a handgun in blasting open the safe. After removing the cash from the safe, all four robbers escaped on foot.

Police estimate the robbers got away with more than $5,000.

The robbery occurred at 1:50 A.M.

3B

(HONOLULU)--James Epperlein, former mayor of Midcity for three terms in the 1940s and 1950s, died here today after a long illness. He was 73.

Elected mayor in 1942 for his first term, Epperlein held the position until 1954, when he was defeated by Margaret Jenkins, Midcity's first woman mayor. Epperlein became the chief executive officer of the First Hawaiian Bank of Honolulu in 1955. He retired from that position in 1975.

The Midcity native graduated from Midcity University in 1932. He was a member of the varsity football team and worked on the student paper, The Daily Tiger.

Epperlein is survived by his wife, Connie, and four children. Services will be held Wednesday in Honolulu at the Sakamoto Mortuary.

3C

(Reporter voicer)

Information:

    Public hearings start tomorrow on the city's proposed $612 million budget. Budget is an 11% increase over last year's, but inflation locally has been running at about 17%. Lots of cuts are expected in programs. Hearings will start at 9 A.M. at the Board of Supervisors chambers, 1700 Burton Lane.

(Reporter Nancy Kim did voicer on probable program cuts.)

VOICER IN: We can expect bumpier roads and "pay for play" tennis courts if all the expected cuts are made.

VOICER OUT: Nancy Kim reporting for K-C-T-I radio news. TIME :30

3D

(MIDCITY)--A local couple was taken into custody today in connection with the poisoning yesterday of four of the five dogs owned by Mrs. Anna Webster, 49, 6392 N. 57th St.
    Paul J. Lowe, 33, 6387 Pike Dr., and Barbara B. Lowe, 31, were booked into Midcity Jail facilities for alleged felony dog poisoning after the Midcity Humane Society executed a warrant signed by Municipal Court Judge William Howatt.
    The Lowes, Webster's back neighbors, face four counts each of felony dog poisoning, Midcity Humane Society Capt. Michael Shirley said today.
    Some meat laced with strychnine was tossed yesterday into Webster's yard where four Afghan hounds and a poodle were kept. Three of the Afghans and the poodle died.

3E

(MIDCITY)--Midcity Fire Capt. Gary J. Spalding, 39, pleaded innocent today before Municipal Court Judge Darlene Chaney on charges of petty theft, receiving stolen property, and carrying a concealed weapon of a loaded gun.
    Craig Gunnersley, defense counsel, and Brenda Kelly, deputy district attorney, agreed to meet next week before setting a preliminary hearing date.
    Spalding has been free on bond since his arrest last month at a home building site in North Midcity. Police, investigating a prowler call, said they found Spalding loading his car with several bags of copper pipe taken from the site.
    Spalding was suspended without pay from the Midcity Fire Department pending the outcome of his trial.

3F

                                                                    NEWS
University News Service   MIDCITY UNIVERSITY
Phone 800-555-5555

                                                          Survey Results #1

A recent poll of Midcity University students shows that despite the complaints often heard about the university, the majority gives MU high evaluations.

Paul J. Strand, director of the MU Poll, reports that 92% of students are satisfied with life in general at the university and 85% are satisfied with the school's community atmosphere.

Location and quality of education are among the most popular features of the university. More than 22% of the students indicated they continue to attend MU because of its location. More than 27% of the students indicated that they continue to attend because of the quality of education that MU provides. When asked whether they were satisfied or dissatisfied with the quality of education here, only 18% of the students indicated any dissatisfaction.

Despite high evaluations, the university does have some drawbacks. More than 67% of the students are dissatisfied with registration. When asked to indicate "which feature of the university would most likely lead you to withdraw," 13% of the students indicated registration and 13% indicated the crowded conditions at MU. Parking, though unpopular, was not considered important enough to warrant withdrawal.

The survey results were based on telephone interviews conducted last month with a scientifically selected sample of 300 students. The margin for error for this survey is approximately 5%.

MU plans to conduct similar polls each semester to keep officials abreast of student attitudes and needs.

                                    ###

3G

(Actuality available)

Information:

Midcity teachers are still on strike. Day #5 for strike of K-12 teachers.

Official Midcity Unified School District reports indicate a 50% attendance rate by students, but the Midcity Teachers Association says the attendance is much lower--closer to 25%.

No violence yet. Atmosphere is relatively calm and friendly on the picket lines in front of schools and the district offices.

Some strikebreakers, but they, so far, are being treated kindly.

Dist. Supt. Eric Otterman reported most of the district's 2,559 teachers remained on strike, but their places have been taken by 1,043 substitute teachers who are being paid $60 per day.

Otterman said the district is pursuing legal action against the MTA, but he would not elaborate further.

The Midcity Board of Education met in special session last night and upped its 8% salary increase offer to 10%. Teacher officials say they intend to hold out for 15%.

The Board of Education has scheduled another special session tonight at Lincoln High School at 7 P.M. in Roan Cafeteria.

Both teacher officials and district officials say the only thing standing in the way of ending the strike is the money impasse.

The average teacher pay in Midcity is $19,900.

(Actuality with Karly Aaron, a teacher who has refused to strike and was on the job today at Hamilton Elementary School. She teaches third grade).

AARON actuality: TIME :20

"I'm one of the few regular teachers still teaching, because the strike is simply against my own personal principles. I cannot compromise my conscience, but my sympathies are completely with my friends and colleagues out on the picket lines. We are severely overworked and underpaid, but I just cannot bring myself to walk out on my students. They need me."

3H

(MIDCITY)--Burglars took an estimated $35,000 worth of jewelry late last night from the "Gem of a Store" boutique in Fashion Square, Midcity police reported.

The thieves bypassed the burglar alarm system by removing a glass panel in a skylight and slipping through the opening in the roof, police said.

The burglary was the third at the boutique in the last two months.

Police have no suspects.

3I

(CHICAGO)--Melinda J. Russell, the so-called "Welfare Queen," who welfare officials report is the biggest welfare chiseler of all time, was sentenced today to 5-10 years in prison.

Miss Russell, alias Linda Russ, Roxanne Lind, Melinda Lindholm, Linda Russe, and others, was convicted last month of theft and perjury.

Prosecuters said the offenses for which she was convicted resulted in her obtaining $97,875.50, but investigators say her schemes, aliases, and disguises were so numerous and intricate that it would be impossible to ascertain precisely how much she bilked welfare agencies out of.

An investigation shows she used her many aliases and disguises to obtain at least $197,498.50 for medical assistance, cash assistance, and bonus cash food stamps, said Walter P. Bickman, director of the Illinois Public Aid Department.

"Miss Russell is without a doubt the biggest welfare cheat of all time," Bickman said. "She's been living the good life at the expense of the government and of the people who really need assistance. I'm glad we got her. I only wish her sentence was heavier."

Russell, 49, refused to talk with reporters after the sentencing.

3J

(CAMPO, CALIF.)--The ad in the "Campo Courier" read, "Chicken, 57¢ a pound."

So, when Brian M. Sayers, 36, opened his "Campo General Store," sheriff's deputies were first in line this morning.

The deputies arrested Sayers and Samuel P. Hall, 28, an employee at the store, and charged them with grand larceny.

Deputies alleged the 5,000 pounds of chicken at Sayers' store came from the 65-crate shipment of chicken that was stolen from the Campo Poultry Works three days ago.

Deputies became suspicious, they said, when chicken worth at least $1.89 a pound was advertised for just 57¢.

Campo is a small farming town of about 3,000 persons. It is 60 miles northeast of San Diego.

3K

(MIDCITY)--A 9-year-old Midcity boy died here today after he fell out of the back of a pickup truck being driven by his father, police reported.

Another young boy died in a separate accident this morning, but his name has not been released pending notification of next of kin.

In the truck accident, Dennis Dean Tappen, Jr., 2541 Bisbee Ave., fell out of the pickup at 7:45 A.M. as it was making a turn from Norwood Street to Roxanne Drive. He was taken to Midcity General Hospital, but died a short time later, police said.

In the other accident, a 7-year-old boy was killed when he was struck by a car. The boy was crossing in the middle of Bevers Street when he was struck by a car driven by Marilyn Kepperman, 34, 2196 Pearl Ave. Kepperman was not cited. The accident occurred at 7:25 A.M.

The boy was taken to Midcity Memorial Hospital, but was pronounced dead en route.

3L

(Actuality available)

(CINCINNATI)--An explosion blamed on coal dust ripped apart a brick
factory here today, injuring 9 employees.

The explosion set off a fire that roared through the building, which
was more than 100 yards long, but the fire was brought under control
quickly.

A spokesman for the Cincinnati Fire Department said one building in
the Meadows and Heighton Co. factory collapsed after the explosion at
8:15 A.M.

The 9 injured workers were taken to Cincinnati General Hospital.
Two were listed in critical condition, two in serious condition and five
in fair condition.

Edward Kaiser, a spokesman for the company, estimated the damage at
more than $1.5 million.

(Actuality with Cincinnati Fire Chief Nelson Bentley.)

BENTLEY actuality: TIME :15

"It looks as if the fire started when some coal dust was ignited by one
of the furnaces in the plant. We got everybody out, though. There were
16 employees in the plant when the explosion occurred and we've accounted
for all 16. It's a real mess, though. That's for sure."

13 / WRITING FOR TELEVISION

ON-CAMERA READER STORIES

Use this example as a model for exercises in this section. The rewritten version is on the next page.

(Original)

(SAN FRANCISCO)--Gerald Kennedy, 66, who was wounded in the invasion of Normandy, June 14, 1944, received his Purple Heart award yesterday. The citation came in the mail, postmarked last week, without any explanation of why it was late. Kennedy is a retired California state employee. He lives in San Francisco.

###

(Rewrite)

purple heart   TRT   :25
smith
3/6/83

TALENT: A San Francisco man received a Purple Heart

                                     award in the mail yesterday. It was a little

                                     late, though.

                                     Gerald Kennedy was wounded during the D-Day

                                     invasion of Normandy on June 14th, 1944.

                                     The citation was postmarked only last week,

                                     so I guess we can't blame the post office folks

                                     this time.

                                     Actually, it's not clear who's at fault.

                                     The award came with no explanation as to why it

                                     was so late.

                                              ###

ON-CAMERA READER #1

Write a :15 on-camera reader story from the following information.

Priscilla Ann Rivers, 38, was killed this morning when she was struck by two cars as she walked on Dole St. near Midcity Community College.
Accident occurred at 9:35 A.M.
Rivers pronounced dead at scene.
Rivers was hit by a car driven by Gary J. Johnson, 20, 1836 May Way, according to police.
Impact of collision threw Rivers into the path of a car going in the opposite direction. Car driven by Alice B. Thomas, 54, 7529 Baxter Dr.
Neither driver was cited.
Death was number 63 in Midcity traffic toll this year.

ON-CAMERA READER #2

Write a :30 on-camera reader story from the following information.

University News Service   NEWS
Phone 800-555-5555   MIDCITY UNIVERSITY

                                                        Sports Terminated #1

Men's and women's swimming will continue as intercollegiate sports at Midcity University, but women's field hockey, men's and women's badminton, and men's water polo will be terminated effective immediately, it was announced today by President Philip Longley.
The move was made in order to utilize limited resources more effectively and provide a better balance to men's and women's programs, Longley added.
The action by Longley came after studying a proposal from the school's department of athletics via the director of athletics, which called for the termination of women's field hockey, men's and women's swimming, men's water polo, and men's and women's badminton.
The approved changes will allow for a modest strengthening of support for volleyball, basketball, gymnastics, and tennis--all major women's sports programs--and for streamlining the women's athletic program, Longley noted.
"Our purpose," Longley remarked, "is to use our resources more effectively. Our ambitions have outstripped our means, though. If we are to achieve the quality we seek, we must limit the number of programs we support."

                                    ###

PICTURE AND SLIDE STORIES (FULL-SCREEN GRAPHICS)

Use this example as a model for the exercises in this section. The rewritten version is on the next page.

In most cases, a still graphic is taken "full screen" for only :12-:15.

(Original)

(HONOLULU)--Computer expert Douglas M. Coe, 31, was arrested here this morning. Coe is accused of stealing $15.2 million from the Bank of Hawaii.

Bank officials say someone used a very complicated computer program to divert the money from various accounts into a numbered Swiss bank account.

Coe worked for the Bank of Hawaii for five years before he resigned last month. His resignation came one week before the computer transfer of funds was discovered.

Coe was arrested this morning at Honolulu International Airport. He was returning from a trip to Los Angeles. He serves as a computer consultant for several small businesses in Los Angeles and San Francisco.

Coe has purchased three expensive new cars in the last two weeks despite earning about $30,000 per year with the Bank of Hawaii.

Coe will be arraigned tomorrow before Circuit Court Judge Roscoe J. Jefferson.

PICTURE: Shows Coe, in handcuffs, being led to police car by officer.

###

(Rewrite)

bank rip-off   TRT :30
mcfadden
6/15/82

TALENT: Honolulu police have arrested a suspect in

                                 that 15-million-dollar rip-off by computer from

                                 the Bank of Hawaii.

TAKE COE PIC   They nabbed 31-year-old Douglas Coe at the

FULL SCREEN   Honolulu International Airport this morning.

                                 Coe had worked for the bank as a computer expert

                                 for five years before resigning last month. A

                                 week after his resignation, the rip-off was

                                 discovered.

TALENT: In the computer scheme, someone diverted

                                 money from accounts at the Bank of Hawaii to a

                                 bank in Switzerland.

                                 Coe will be arraigned tomorrow.

                                            ###

FULL-SCREEN GRAPHIC #1

   Write a :30 television news story from the following information.
Use the picture of the smoke bomb exploding for :12.

(SEATTLE)--A bank robber here got more than he bargained for this morning. Paul B. Canfield, 36, robbed the Northwest Federal Savings and Loan
branch in downtown Seattle of $57,000.
   Canfield got out of the bank with the money without much trouble.
He stuffed the money into pockets in his pants and coat and made his
escape on foot.
   Canfield ran into a nearby department store, but there his luck ran
out. While in the store, his pants and coat exploded in a cloud of bil-
lowing red smoke. It seems a teller, who gave Canfield the money, also
gave him explosive money packets containing tear gas and red dye.
   As startled bystanders looked on, the suspect dashed into a restroom
with smoke gushing from the pockets of his slacks and coat.
   Police were alerted and they arrested Canfield. He was not injured.

PICTURE: Shows Canfield waving arms to dispel smoke; people staring at
           him in background.

FULL-SCREEN GRAPHIC #2

   Write a :30 television news story from the following information.
Use the map of the earthquake epicenter for :12.

Information:

   Big quake in Southern California this afternoon.
   No deaths or injuries reported. Plenty of property damage, though.
   Officials at the California Civil Defense Department estimate the
damage at $2 million.
   Quake measured 7.6 on the Richter Scale.
   Earthquake experts at the University of California-San Diego have
indicated the epicenter of the quake was about 6 miles east of Santee,
California, a suburb of San Diego. They expect aftershocks throughout
the night tonight and all day tomorrow.
   Quake hit at 2:38 P.M. California time.
   Quake felt in Los Angeles, San Diego, and surrounding cities.

PICTURE: Map that shows location of epicenter. On map is Santee, San
           Diego, Los Angeles, Palm Springs, and a large "X" marking the
           epicenter.

PRE-EDITED FILM AND VIDEOTAPE STORIES

Use this example as a model for the exercises in this section. The
rewritten version is on the next page.

(Original)

Information:

Fire at a warehouse in downtown Midcity. Warehouse owned by Fast-
Gro Company, a fertilizer manufacturing company. No fertilizer in building, though, just a bunch of machinery for packaging it. It was outdated
equipment that was just being stored.

Twenty-five firemen on the scene for most of the time. Fire started
about noon and lasted until 3 P.M. No injuries. Damage estimate is
$185,000. Building's a total loss. Cleanup operations lasted until
5 P.M. The 2-story warehouse was approximately 55 years old.

Fire Capt. John Luter (LOO-ter) said an electrical short was the
cause of the fire. The short ignited some gasoline soaked rags. Luter
gave the damage estimate, too.

A warehouse for Tire Town, a local automobile tire store chain, was
in danger for a while. The warehouse is next door to the one that burned
down. Some tires were rolled out, but when the all clear was given,
workers started rolling the tires back in.

Shot List:

1.	Cover--flames, firemen, fire trucks	:06
2.	Medium shot of Luter	:03
3.	Medium shot of firemen spraying water	:05
4.	Medium shot of flames	:05
5.	Close-up of fire truck	:03
6.	Medium shot of workers rolling tires	:05
7.	Cover--mop up and more tire rolling	:06
	TOTAL	:33

(Rewrite)

fertilizer fire   TRT :45
wulfemeyer
6/15/82

TALENT:	Fire destroyed a fertilizer warehouse in downtown Midcity this afternoon.
TAKE SIL FILM/VO :06	Nobody was hurt, but the fire caused about 185-thousand-dollars damage. Fire Captain John (LOO-ter) Luter said the blaze started when an electrical short ignited some gasoline-soaked rags. The fire started about noon and burned until three. Cleanup work lasted until five. In all, 25 firemen battled the blaze. For a time, the Tire Town warehouse next door was in danger and some tires were rolled out as a precaution, but when the all clear was given, workmen started rolling the tires back in.
:21	
TALENT:	The fertilizer warehouse is owned by the Fast-Gro Company. There wasn't any fertilizer in the warehouse, though, just some old equipment.

###

DISCUSSION:

Before beginning to write the script, the writer read the information and then looked at the "shot list." Most of the scenes were of the fire and firefighting, but at :06 into the film, the fire captain appeared. Luter would have to be mentioned at approximately :06, so the information would have to be organized to match that point.

The only other specific matching point, the writer determined, was the scene of workers rolling tires. The scene started at :22 into the voice over, so information would have to be ordered to permit matching.

Take a look at the model script. Notice how when the scene of Luter appears, the anchor is talking about him and when the scene of the tire rolling appears, the anchor is talking about it. Strive for this kind of audio and video matching.

Use the general scenes in the film or videotape to explain the details of the event or issue.

VIDEO SCRIPT #1

Write a :30 "voice over" script using the following information and film scenes. The film has already been edited. Write your script to match it. Be sure to include a brief on-camera lead and tail.   TRT :45

Information (from Midcity police officers at scene):
Two-car traffic accident at the corner of 54th St. and Western Blvd. Three local people involved. Driver of one car died at scene--Glen Peterson, 4523 Niagara Ave. Passenger in Peterson's car--Anita Swann, 510 State St., was not hurt.

Driver of other car, Henry W. Coleman, 831 Hamilton Dr., not injured, but arrested--charge, manslaughter. Witnesses said Coleman ran a stop sign and smashed into the side of Peterson's car.

Information (from Dep. County Coroner, Maria Lopez):
Peterson died from multiple head injuries caused when his head hit the door on the driver's side.

Information (from photographer):
Coleman frisked by police. Kept saying, "I didn't see the stop sign. I didn't see it. It was hidden by a tree branch."

Information (obtained from Midcity police information officer):
Accident occurred at 7:45 A.M. today. Coleman booked on felony manslaughter charges. Taken to Midcity Correctional Center. Bail set at $50,000. Peterson was 29; Swann, 24; and Coleman, 44.

Shot List:

1.	Cover--cars, police, people	:05
2.	Medium shot of covered body	:04
3.	Close-up of Swann crying	:03
4.	Medium shot police questioning Coleman	:06
5.	Medium shot of stop sign and tree	:05
6.	Cover--cars, police, people	:10
	TOTAL	:33

VIDEO SCRIPT #2

Write a :45 "voice over" script from the following information and
videotape scenes. The videotape has already been edited. Write your
script to match it. Include an on-camera lead and tail.   TRT 1:00

University News Service   NEWS
Phone 800-555-5555   MIDCITY UNIVERSITY

                                                      Windmills #1

    Students interested in wind power have come to Midcity University
from all over the state to learn more about windmills. They are taking
part in a special MU Extension Services course, "Windmill Technology."
It will run two weeks.
    The course is the first of its kind offered in the United States.
It started today and consists of 40 hours of lectures and field experience per week. Twenty-five students are taking the course. They were
selected from approximately 175 who applied.
    The course is designed to fill the needs of rural communities where
qualified windmill technicians are practically nonexistent. Subject
material will include history, design, repair, maintenance, and installation of wind-powered machinery for pumping water and generating electric-
ity.
    The instructor for the course, Roger Litton, has been in the wind-
mill business for 35 years.
    "The increasing costs of electricity has really increased the
interest in windmills," he said. "I look at the course as the university's contribution to the country's energy-saving program."
    The United Nations has even sent an observer to monitor the course
to see if it might be used to train technicians for third world countries.
    Tuition for the course is $300. Additional courses are planned in
future semesters and reservations are already coming in.
    For more information, contact the MU News Service.
    Shot List:
            1. Cover--students, instructor, building site   :08
            2. Close-up of a student looking at blueprint   :05
            3. Medium shot of windmill blades on ground   :05
            4. Medium shot of Litton   :10
            5. Medium shot of students working   :08
            6. Medium shot of UN observer   :05
            7. Cover--students working, windmill   :07
                                         TOTAL   :48

UNEDITED FILM AND VIDEOTAPE STORIES

Use this example as a model for the exercises in this section. The rewritten version is on the next page.

(Original)

Information:

Two West Midcity men are raising buffalo on their 40-acre ranch. Men released their herd to the open pasture today for the first time. Theodore ("Ted") McFadden and Bartholomew ("Bart") Bascomb bought the buffalo, 30 head, in South Dakota. They paid $60,000 for the herd.
Men say raising buffalo is better than cattle for several reasons.
1. Eat weeds and scrub brush and bushes that cattle wouldn't touch.
2. Are heartier--they can stand cold and heat better.
3. Have more meat on them.
Mac says there are some problems with buffalo, though.
1. Are harder to handle than cattle because they're temperamental and excitable.
2. Need stronger fences, because they're stronger than cattle.
3. Meat is more expensive than beef--average of 28¢ per pound more than beef on all cuts.
Mac says less fat on buffalo, though, and buffalo meat tastes better than beef. Men plan to sell buffalo meat to restaurants in Midcity, NOT to retail stores or markets.

Shot List:

1.	Cover--buffalo in meadow	:15
2.	Men talking in meadow (medium shot)	:10
3.	McFadden dalking (close-up)	:10
4.	Bascomb talking (close-up)	:10
5.	Buffalo in meadow eating grass	:15
6.	Various shots of buffalo (close-ups)	:20
	TOTAL	:80

(Rewrite)

buffalo   TRT :50
bliss
7/14/82

TALENT: Some buffalo have found a home on the range in

                     West Midcity.

TAKE SIL FILM/VO   Thirty buffalo have started roaming around the

:03   40-acre ranch that belongs to Ted McFadden and

:06   Bart Bascomb. The men imported their herd from

:09   South Dakota after paying 60-thousand-dollars for it.

:12   McFadden and Bascomb say they decided to try buffalo

:15   instead of beef for three reasons:

:17   Buffalo eat weeds and scrub brush that beef won't

:20   touch...buffalo can stand heat and cold better...and

:23   there's more meat on buffalo.

:25   McFadden says there are a few drawbacks to raising

:28   buffalo, though. They're more temperamental than beef

:31   and they need stronger fences. Buffalo meat also costs

:34   about 28-cents a pound more than beef, but McFadden

:37   thinks it has less fat and tastes better than beef.

TALENT: McFadden and Bascomb are going to sell their buffalo

                     meat only to local restaurants, so you won't be able to

                     find it at any local market.

Shot List:
          1. Cover of buffalo   :12
          2. Men talking   :15
          3. Buffalo eating   :08
          4. McFadden close-up   :05
          5. Buffalo close-ups   :13
                                 TOTAL :43

DISCUSSION:

    After the writer had produced the script for the story, the available video was edited to match the audio. The copy ran about :40, so the video had to run :43. Most of the scenes were pretty general, but the script was reasonably general, too.

    The video and audio had to match exactly at just two spots: the scene of the two men talking needed to be placed to match the mention of them giving reasons for picking buffalo, and the close-up of McFadden needed to be placed to match the mention of him giving the negative aspects of buffalo raising.

    The mention of their talking starts at :12 into the script, so :12 of video had to be placed before the scene of them talking. McFadden is quoted at :25 into the script, so the close-up of him had to appear then. To achieve the desired matching, the rest of the video scenes were edited-in before and after the specific matching points.

    Look at how this was done. The scenes could have been put together in other ways, but the important thing is to have the video match the audio as closely as possible.

    In the exercises in this section, avoid editing any scene to be shorter than :03. Anything shorter than :03 is too short for most viewers to make much sense of it.

    Be sure to include the running time of your script in the left margin. This wouldn't be done at many stations, but it will help your instructor evaluate your editing.

VIDEO WRITING AND EDITING #1

Write a :30 "voice over" script from the following information and video scenes. After you write your story, edit the videotape to match your copy. You may arrange the scenes in any order and you may shorten any scene; however, you may NOT lengthen any scene. Include an on-camera lead and tail. TRT :45

Information (from MAALA spokesperson):

Big antique car auction last night. '29 Duesenberg brought $175,000. It was a model J, owned by Sara M. Flint (Los Angeles). Bought by Randolph T. Harris (Denver). It was the 5th highest price in history paid for a car at a public auction.

Auction was part of National Association of Antique and Classic Car Clubs of North America convention. Convention being held at the Town and Country Hotel in Midcity. Auction held in hotel's "Monarch Room."

More than $3,000,000 bid at auction. 550 bidders from every state, Canada, and Mexico. 2,500 people watched auction.

Second highest price paid last night was for a '34 Duesenberg. M. T. Terpin (Des Moines) sold it to Warren L. Kenning (Dallas) for $128,000.

Bargain of the night was a '49 VW Beetle. It sold for only $3,250.

No Midcity buyers or sellers. Pres. of Midcity Antique Auto Lovers Association (MAALA), Jeffrey W. Ryan, said, "The bidding was a bit rich for any of our members and we didn't have anyone who wanted to part with his car."

Convention ends tomorrow. Cars on display and open to public from 10 A.M. to 10 P.M.

Shot List: (NOTE--You should have :33 of "edited" videotape)

1.	Cover--cars, bidders, audience	:10
2.	Medium shot of '29 Dusie with new owner	:10
3.	Close-up of Harris	:05
4.	Medium shot of audience	:10
5.	Medium shot of bidders	:10
6.	Close-up of auctioneer	:05
7.	Medium shot of '49 VW	:10
8.	Medium shot of '34 Dusie and new owner	:10
	TOTAL	:70

VIDEO WRITING AND EDITING #2

Write a :45 "voice over" script from the following information and video scenes. The film should be edited to match your copy. Include an on-camera lead and tail. TRT 1:00

Information:

(MIDCITY)--Two local men, knocked to the ground by a runaway vintage airplane, were pulled to safety as the aircraft ran wildly in an elliptical pattern for 15 minutes at Midcity Municipal Airport at 8:35 A.M.

The men, William Vernon, the owner of the plane, and Robert Knox, were working on the engine of the Ryan PT-22 when the airplane jumped the wheel blocks and began to spin in an "erratic" fashion and presented a serious hazard until it crashed into a twin-engine Bonanza near the hangar section, according to Richard Allen, airport operations manager.

Vernon and Knox were knocked to the airstrip when they attempted to halt the aircraft and both were stunned and semiconscious as the plane whirled in an unpredictable pattern.

Pilots and mechanics at the airport pulled the two men from the path of the unmanned plane.

The World War II plane finally crashed into the Bonanza owned by the Tibbs Flying Service and came to a halt, Allen said.

Vernon and Knox were transported to Midcity General Hospital and were released after receiving treatment for contusions and lacerations to the head and body.

Both the trainer plane (PT-22) and the Bonanza were heavily damaged as the wooden propeller of the PT-22 ground into the side of the twin-engine aircraft and came to a halt.

Shot List: (You will need :48 of "edited" film.)
            1.   Cover--planes hooked together   :15
            2.   Medium shot of men (Vernon on right)   :10
            3.   Close-up of propeller stuck in plane   :10
            4.   Medium shot of men being treated at scene :10
            5.   Cover--workers trying to separate planes :20
                                              TOTAL   :65

Remember: You may arrange the scenes in any order and may shorten any scene, but you may NOT lengthen any scene. Be sure to give the running time of your script in the left margin. Take a look at the model story, if you need to refresh yourself on the format.

SOUND BITE INTRODUCTIONS

Use this example as a model for the exercises in this section. The rewritten version is on the next page.

(Original)

Information:

A theft at Midcity University. Someone copped an APPLE microcomputer from the university's Computer Instructional Laboratory this morning. Value of unit set at $5,500. Midcity police have no leads.

Lawrence Matthews, dir. of computer facilities at MU, reported the room which housed the computer and 13 computer terminals was locked, but the locks had been broken.

The microcomputer was used to acquaint business students with its advanced technology.

MATTHEWS SOUND BITE: TIME :20

"It's a real mystery. The APPLE is a nice little computer, but we have a lot more valuable equipment in the lab that wasn't even touched. The sad thing really is that we won't be able to replace the unit this year. We're going to install better locks, though, and we're adding an alarm system, too. This isn't going to happen to us again."

(Rewrite)

computer rip-off   TRT :45
wulfemeyer
9/30/82

TALENT: Midcity University will have to do without

                               one of its computers this year. Someone broke

                               into the school's computer laboratory this

                               morning and made off with a 55-hundred-dollar

                               APPLE microcomputer.

                               The Director of Computer Facilities at

                               Midcity U., Larry Matthews, is a little puzzled

                               about why just the APPLE computer was taken.

TAKE SOT   IN: "It's a real mystery..."

                                                      TIME: :20

                               OUT: "...happen to us again."

SUPER: MATTHEWS
00:00-00:10

TALENT: The computer was used mostly by business

                               students. There are no leads in the case so far.

SOUND BITE #1

Write a :15 introduction from the following information to set up the sound bite. TRT :30

Information:

State Senator Lester Murakami (D-Midcity) is smiling today. His bill to provide $350,000 for a new park in Midcity was signed by Gov. John Sorenson this morning.

Construction at the Jackson Drive site in East Midcity should begin early next month.

Murakami is up for reelection this year. He is running against lawyer Lucille Edwards, a republican.

Park will feature softball diamonds, a children's playground, and restrooms.

MURAKAMI SOUND BITE: TIME :15

"Well, I'm very happy, of course. We need that park. It took a little bit of lobbying on my part, but it was worth it. I hope the park will be only the beginning of the revitalization process for East Mid-city."

SOUND BITE #2

Write a brief lead and tail from the following information for the sound bite. TRT :45

Information:

Unemployment is up in Midcity for the 9th straight month.

Rate climbed to 6.7% of the work force last month. The month before it was 6.3%.

There were 49,200 men and women out of work last month compared to 46,800 the month before.

Last year for the same month, the jobless rate was 5.8%.

Midcity Chamber of Commerce is going to hold a press conference tomorrow to discuss ways to combat the growing unemployment.

Sound bite is with Billie Jean Miller, director of the Midcity C of C.

MILLER SOUND BITE: TIME :18

"The job situation in Midcity is pretty bad right now and it could get worse. There just aren't enough jobs to go around right now and with money getting tighter, the job situation could get even uglier. We're hoping to try a couple of things locally that might stimulate the economy."

REPORTER PACKAGE INTRODUCTIONS

Use this example as a model for the exercises in this section. The rewritten version is on the next page.

(Original)

Information:

First day of garbage workers strike. Picketers out in force this morning in front of the Department of Sanitation garage.

Brief confrontation between workers and management personnel who attempted to cross picket line. No injuries. Just a lot of pushing and name calling.

No negotiation session was scheduled for today, but a session is set for tomorrow at 8 A.M.

Workers want a pay hike of 15%, but the city has offered just 7%.

The average garbage worker earns $23,500.

Lorin Kelly covered the story for KCTI.

KELLY OPENING: The picketers were all from Public Employees
                 Local 3-4-5.

KELLY OUT: Kelly for KCTI News.   TIME: 1:15

###

(Rewrite)

garbage strike   TRT 1:30
kelly
8/4/82

TALENT: Garbage workers were out on the picket line

                                 this morning and K-C-T-I's Lorin Kelly was out

                                 there, too.

_____

TAKE SOT   IN: "The picketers were all...:

                                                        TIME: 1:15

                                 OUT: "Kelly for KCTI News."

_____

TALENT: The garbage workers are asking for a 15

                                 percent pay increase, but the city wants to give

                                 them only seven percent.

                                 Negotiations will resume tomorrow morning.

                                          ###

Reporter Package #1

Write a :15 introduction from the following information for the reporter package. None of the information provided is included in the
package. TRT 1:45

Information:

More bad news on the housing front. The average price for a single-
family home in Midcity is now $135,000, according to the Midcity Realtors
Association. Last year at this time the average price was $115,000.
The high cost has put a dent in the local real estate business.
Sales on single-family homes are down 35% from just six months ago and
are down 50% from a year ago.
KCTI reporter Mollie Smith covered the story. She and her husband,
Gary, bought a new home two weeks ago.

SMITH OPENING: A lot of Midcity residents are being priced right
                  out of the single-family housing market these days.

SMITH OUT: Smith, KCTI News, East Midcity.   TIME: 1:30

Reporter Package #2

Write a lead and tail from the following information for the reporter package. None of the information provided is included in the
package. TRT 1:30

Information:

Attendance at Midcity Zoo is up from last year. Latest figures show
1.5 million persons have visited the zoo so far this year, compared to
1.3 million persons at this time last year.
All of the different and exotic animals are the major attractions,
but KCTI reporter Kevin Cooney has done a story about another part of the
zoo. He found out that there are over 200,000 different varieties of
plants and flowers at the zoo. Some are extremely rare and valuable. In
fact, the plants and flowers at the zoo are worth more than the animals.
The animals are worth about $5,000,000 and the plants and flowers about
$5,500,000, according to zoo officials.

COONEY OPENING: You can find crowds like this every day here at
                  the Midcity Zoo.

COONEY OUT: Cooney for KCTI News.   TIME: 1:00

APPENDIX

A. NAMES PRONUNCIATION GUIDE

Beaton, Jan	(BEE-tuhn)	Loren, Donna	(LOHR-ehn)
Beetow, Theodore	(BEE-toh)	Lowe, Paul	(LOH)
Castillo, Jose	(Kas-TEE-oh, HOH-zay)	Nater, Pamela	(NAY-ter)
Castro, Alonzo	(KAS-troh)	O'Keefe, James	(OH-keef)
Dantly, Teri	(DANT-lee)	Otterman, Eric	(AHT-ter-muhn)
Epperlein, James	(EHP-per-leyen)	Reeger, Jane	(REE-ger)
Ester, Karl	(EHS-ter)	Sakamoto, Gloria	(SAHK-ah-moh-toh)
Gunnersley, Craig	(GUHN-ners-lee)	Sanchez, Maria	(SAN-chehz)
Hedgeman, Roger	(HEHDG-muhn)	Sennett, Charles	(SEHN-neht)
Katz, Marvin	(KATS)	Taite, William	(TAYT)
Kiperts, Donald	(KIH-perts)		

Note: Your instructor will provide correct pronunciation for names that do not appear here.

B. READING LIST

The following books will help you in your study of broadcast news.

Bittner, John R., and Bittner, Denise A. *Radio Journalism*. Englewood Cliffs, N.J.: Prentice-Hall, 1977.

Bliss, Edward, Jr., and Patterson, John M. *Writing News for Broadcast*. New York: Columbia University Press, 1978.

Broussard, E. Joseph, and Holgate, Jack F. *Writing and Reporting Broadcast News*. New York: Macmillan, 1982.

Fang, Irving E. *Television News*. St. Paul, Minn.: Rada Press, 1980.

Garvey, Daniel E., and Rivers, William L. *Newswriting for the Electronic Media*. Belmont, Calif.: Wadsworth, 1982.

Shook, Frederick, and Lattimore, Dan. *The Broadcast News Process*. Denver, Colo.: Morton, 1979.

Stephens, Mitchell. *Broadcast News*. New York: Holt, Rinehart and Winston, 1980.

Wulfemeyer, K. Tim. *Beginning Broadcast Newswriting: A Self-Instructional Learning Experience*. Ames: Iowa State University Press, 1976.

K. TIM WULFEMEYER teaches mass communication at the University of Hawaii-Manoa, with a special emphasis on broadcast news production and reporting. He is widely published in the journals of his field, and besides this book is author of *Beginning Broadcast Newswriting: A Self-Instructional Learning Experience* (1976). He holds the master's degree from Iowa State University, Ames, and a doctorate in higher education from the University of California, Los Angeles. His research centers on the content of television newscasts and how students can best be prepared for careers in broadcast journalism.